The Shetland Bus

Transporting Secret Agents Across the North Sea in WW2

The Shetland Bus

Transporting Secret Agents Across the North Sea in WW2

Stephen Wynn

Pen & Sword
MILITARY

AN IMPRINT OF PEN & SWORD BOOKS LTD.
YORKSHIRE - PHILADELPHIA

First published in Great Britain in 2021 by
Pen & Sword Military
An imprint of
Pen & Sword Books Ltd
Yorkshire - Philadelphia

ISBN 978 1 52673 535 5

A CIP catalogue record for this book is available from the British Library.

Printed and bound in England
By CPI Group (UK) Ltd, Croydon, CR0 4YY

Pen & Sword Books Ltd. incorporates the Imprints of Pen & Sword
Archaeology, Atlas, Aviation, Battleground, Discovery, Family History,
History, Maritime, Military, Naval, Politics, Railways, Select, Transport,
True Crime, Fiction, Frontline Books, Leo Cooper, Praetorian Press,
Seaforth Publishing, Wharncliffe and White Owl.

For a complete list of Pen & Sword titles please contact

PEN & SWORD BOOKS LIMITED
47 Church Street, Barnsley, South Yorkshire, S70 2AS, England
E-mail: enquiries@pen-and-sword.co.uk
Website: www.pen-and-sword.co.uk

or

PEN AND SWORD BOOKS
1950 Lawrence Rd, Havertown, PA 19083, USA
E-mail: uspen-and-sword@casematepublishers.com
Website: www.penandswordbooks.com

Contents

Acknowledgements

I would like to say a big thank you to Gaynor Haliday for her time, effort, patience and understanding in the editing of this book. Her work on it will undoubtedly enhance the experience of whoever reads it.

Introduction

Shetland comprises a group of small islands, sixteen of which are inhabited, situated 110 miles off of the Scottish mainland in the Northern Atlantic, between Great Britain and Norway, which is some 190 miles away to the west. Due to their remote location, life on the islands can be harsh.

The islands have been inhabited since the Mesolithic period, which, in archaeological terms, was between the Upper Paleolithic and Neolithic periods. It was a period that saw Shetland dominated by Scandanavian influences, especially Norwegian, and in fact it was not until the fifteenth century that the islands became part of Scotland, which in turn did not become part of the United Kingdom until 1707. It was from this time that the decrease in the islands' trade with northern Europe can be traced, leaving fishing as an important aspect of its economy.

One of the links that connects Shetland with its Norse heritage is known as the 'Up Helly Aa', which is a fire festival involving a torchlit procession. There are twelve in total, taking place between January and March every year, each of which culminates in the burning of a Viking galley ship. The main event takes place in Shetland's capital, Lerwick, at the end of January.

The islands' motto is *'Meo logum skal land byggja',* the origins of which can be found in Norwegian heritage, and means *'By law shall land be built'.*

As there have been links between Scotland and the Nordic countries going back over the centuries, the connection between the two locations run deep. Therefore the collaboration between

Shetland and Norway during the course of the Second World War, with the Shetland Bus operation, may be seen as a continuation of a long-standing relationship.

This book will look in more detail at that relationship, the men and boats involved, and the operations carried out until Norway was liberated from German occupation in May 1945.

CHAPTER ONE

Shetland's Role in the Second World War

For some unexplained reason, six German aircraft carried out an attack on Lerwick in November 1939; their target being the harbour. But despite the aircraft dropping a total of eight bombs, they caused very little in the way of damage. The raid was so quick and unexpected there had not even been enough time for the home defences to sound the air raid siren. Where their bombs failed, their machine guns made up for it by strafing a flying boat that was sitting in the harbour. Miraculously, all crew on board at the time survived, despite the aircraft bursting into flames.

The air raid could have resulted in a lot more damage, as there were numerous other vessels in the harbour and just outside of its walls, but they all escaped unscathed.

However, it was the German invasion of Norway rather than the Lerwick attack of November 1939 that resulted in the islands' defences being improved by the British government.

When Germany invaded Norway in April 1940, it created a fear that she might also consider invading Britain via Shetland, rather than the more obvious route of the English Channel. Prior to this point, no such major attack had ever been considered, but after the fall of Norway the British government seriously had to reconsider its position. Shetland's distant position in the far-off reaches of Scotland, where for long periods of the year it was closeted by inclement weather, meant living there was not for the faint-hearted. It was largely because of this environment that there were very few defensive positions in place and even fewer military personnel to deal with any kind of German invasion, especially a full-blown one.

Once the decision had been made to fortify Shetland, it was not long before troopships carrying large numbers of men began arriving. As many as 20,000 British troops were stationed there at any one time, garrisoned at Lerwick, Scalloway, Sumburgh and Sullom Voe; their numbers greater than the inhabitants of Shetland.

Despite the potentially harsh weather conditions that were likely to be encountered by the British troops, they were initially expected to live in tents. Thankfully, the military hierarchy eventually saw sense and the tented accommodation was quickly replaced by Nissen huts.

Improvements to the islands' defences included many of the buildings being protected against bomb blasts, by being surrounded with sandbags. Anti-aircraft guns and artillery pieces were installed in and around the harbour at Lerwick and elsewhere.

But it was not just soldiers who had been hastily moved to one of the furthest military outposts of Britain. Pilots and other air and ground crews of the RAF also found themselves suddenly stationed in the Shetlands, flying and looking after Spitfires and Hurricanes, after new runways had been built at Sumburgh and Scatsta, so that Shetland could be defended from any German air raids. There was also a massive base at Sullom Voe for flying boats. Estimations suggest at one time there were some 1,800 servicemen stationed there: 1,200 British and some 600 Norwegians.

Shetland had suddenly become an important military location as far as the British were concerned. So much so that it became what was known as a restricted military area; in essence nobody was allowed in or out without an official pass.

The full-time forces were supported by Shetland's own Home Guard, who did their bit by carrying out guard and sentry duties at such places as the pier, the Knab and the dockyards.

Shetland and Norway begin their collaboration

A combination of Germany's invasion and subsequent occupation of Norway, along with the oppressive stance they took towards Norwegians, led to the numerous escapes from the country to Shetland.

The British government knew that a number of Norwegian soldiers had avoided capture and were still at large and prepared to fight in an effort to free their nation from the Nazi tyranny. Even in defeat, they were still an army, all they needed were arms, communications, explosives and other relevant equipment, to once again make them into an effective fighting force.

After seeing the large number of Norwegian refugees who had arrived in Shetland, the idea of putting such a unit together was raised. It was realised that if the captains of these relatively small fishing vessels could navigate their way across the North Sea to help others escape from Norway, they could certainly 'retrace their steps' back to Norway with men and equipment, to effectively continue the fight against the occupying forces of Nazi Germany.

As the momentum of this plan gathered speed, it was determined that a base was needed in Shetland where those Norwegian soldiers who had made good their escape could be properly trained as agents. It might sound a strange thing to say that Norwegian, along with British soldiers, needed training before they were sent to Norway, but it has to be remembered that these men were not going to be deployed as infantry soldiers, but as resistance fighters who required guerrilla tactics to fight against their enemy. They needed knowledge in communications and had to know their way round a radio set that could transmit and receive messages. They needed to know how to set up and make bombs that could be used to destroy railway lines and German communication lines, and 'booby' traps that could be used in any number of ways, in an attempt at keep the Germans, 'on their toes'. They had to be able to get up close to an enemy and kill him quickly and without noise, and they had to be able to live off the land if needs be. These were all skills that many did not have, nor had previously wanted to acquire: they may well have been experienced soldiers, but they were total beginners when it came to being agents sent into the midst of the enemy.

The beginnings of the Shetland Bus

Lunna is in the north-east of Shetland and it was to here that those individuals who were to be part of the Shetland Bus operation were sent to undergo their training, before they were taken across the North Sea to Norway to put their training into practice. Lunna was an ideal location for such a secret base as it was tucked out of the way of prying eyes and from any main shipping area, but after a year, the unit moved from Lunna to Scalloway, where a local engineering firm was based. It even had a royal visitor in October 1942; Prince Olaf of Norway, who came to the base to officially open the new base's slipway.

In those early months of operations, it was not plain sailing for the Shetland Bus. The journeys involved the sailing of relatively small boats, usually Norwegian fishing vessels. They were on average between 50 and 70ft in length, had two masts and were driven by a 30 to 70hp single-cylinder semi-diesel engine and operated during the hours of darkness, mainly during the winter months, across the rough and unforgiving waters of the North Sea. If a boat got into difficulties, those on board simply had to get on with it. Nobody was likely to come to their rescue if it all went wrong, and survival in the brutally cold waters would have been for no more than a few minutes at best. There was nothing pleasant about these journeys.

There were losses in both boats and men. Six vessels were either sunk or captured by German forces, whilst others were lost due to atrocious weather conditions, and more than thirty men were killed in the attacks, later died of their wounds, or drowned. It was decided that their best form of defence for these vessels was for them to be decked out to look like a working fishing vessel, and any people out on deck were dressed as fishermen.

Things became so bad that because of the losses there was even talk of the Shetland Bus being closed down. But its officers and men were certainly not prepared to give up without a fight. Their response was typical of such a group. They asked for better equipment to do the job that they were being asked to do. In essence, proper boats to do the job. It had always been a bone of contention amongst many of the men: that the ageing fishing vessels that they had used, and had been expected to use, were simply not up to the task. Too much emphasis had been placed on the fact that these were the very boats that had initially been used to take refugees out of Norway. But the reason these vessels had been used was simple: they were all that was available. There was no fleet of naval quality, well-built, high-speed vessels ready and available for the task, although later in the conflict better boats were provided by the USA.

What was impressive about the Shetland Bus operation was that not only did it provide a way of infiltrating agents into Norway, but it also provided a much-needed escape route for Norwegians wanting to flee the country. It became the lifeblood of the islands' resistance fighters, allowing them to fight back against the occupying Germans. Members of the Special Operations Executive (SOE), the forerunner of the SAS, joined the Norwegians in their fight.

The men who traversed these waters did so for the people of Norway and for the benefit of mankind. These were extremely brave individuals, just by being prepared to even make the journey in the first place. Not only was it one of uncertainty, but once they arrived in Norway there was no way of knowing if their mission had been compromised, and rather than being met by a friendly face with a warm blanket and a cup of tea, they were going to be shot or captured by a group of waiting German soldiers.

After the war the Norwegian authorities issued a number of medals for both Norwegians and allied military personnel, who had undertaken war time service in support of the nation. These were:

St Olav's Medal: awarded in recognition of 'outstanding services rendered in connection with the spreading of information about Norway abroad and for strengthening the bonds between expatriate Norwegians and their home country'.

The Norwegian War Medal: awarded to Norwegian and foreign members of the military who in a meritorious way participated in the Second World War for Norway. The War Medal was also awarded posthumously to all Norwegians and foreigners who fought in the Norwegian forces and merchant marines, or who died whilst fighting for the Norwegian Resistance.

The Defence Medal 1940–1945: awarded to those military and civilian personnel who took part in the fight against the German invasion and occupation of Norway between 1940 and 1945.

CHAPTER TWO

The German Invasion of Norway, 1940

The German invasion of neutral Norway began on 9 April 1940 and ended two months later on 10 June, making it the second longest resistance against a Nazi invasion throughout the course of the Second World War. The obvious question is why did Germany decide to invade a country that had declared itself as being neutral? I will come on to that a little bit later.

The occupation of Norway continued until the surrender of Nazi Germany in May 1945. The Norwegian government, along with the country's King Haakon VII and his family, managed to escape to London where they became a 'government in exile'. The reality was that they had little or no control of what happened in their homeland during their exile in London. The new man in charge of Norway was Josef Antonius Heinrich Terboven, a German and devout Nazi who had the title of *Reichskomissar*, which was a German title used for various public offices during the Second World War.

Josef Terboven had served in the German military with both the Field Artillery and the Air Force during the First World War, eventually rising to the rank of lieutenant. He was also awarded the Iron Cross for bravery. He was a popular figure within the Nazi party, and in 1934 he married Ilse Stahl, who had been the former secretary and lover of Josef Goebbels. One of those present at the wedding was none other than Adolf Hitler, which was a reflection of just how highly thought of Terboven was.

Terboven's role was somewhat of a strange one in relation to Germany's control of the country. The nation's day-to-day affairs were, in essence, run by a Norwegian state administration, led by politician Vidkun Quisling, which was nothing more than a pro-Nazi puppet government. It was under his leadership that the Norwegians assisted the Germans in rounding up members of the nation's Jewish population for deportation to Germany.

Terboven did not have control over any of the 400,000 German troops who were stationed in Norway during the war, instead they came under the command of Genraloberst Nikolaus von Falkenhorst. He did, however, have a personal force of some 6,000 men under his command. An interesting point of note was the widely different approach of Falkenhorst and Terboven. The latter of the two men was somewhat of a bully, who over time became equally disliked by both the Norwegian population and a number of German soldiers. This situation was compounded by the fact that Falkenhorst had ordered his men to treat the Norwegian population with courtesy and respect, which was in keeping with Nazi edicts of the time, as they had no desire to alienate the German soldiers in the eyes of the Norwegian population.

Despite the official mumblings about not wishing to damage relationships between German soldiers and the Norwegian population, when, in December 1944, Falkenhorst opposed a number of what he saw as radical proposals which had been proposed by Terboven, he was sacked.

After Admiral Donitz became the new president of the German Reich in April 1945, he sacked Terboven, replacing him with General Franz Böhme.

It would be fair to describe Terboven as rather a complicated and troubled character, who was a Nazi through and through. A man who had bought into the regime's ideology, hook, line, and sinker. In 1941 he had a concentration camp built at Falstad, in the village of Ekne, near Levanger. Bredtveit prison in Oslo was used by the Nazi collaborationist party, Nasjonal Samling, as a political prison from 1941. After the war it was used to hold women who were awaiting trial for collaborating with German occupying forces. It is still a women's prison to this day.

Falstad began life as a prison camp in September 1941, with the intention that its inmates would be political prisoners, but by the end of the war it is estimated that approximately 4,500 military personnel from thirteen different countries had been incarcerated there.

Such establishments as the University of Oslo had a number of its senior staff members arrested and sent to Bredtveit in October 1943. Earlier that same year a group of Jewish people arrived in Oslo as prisoners. They were also sent to Bredtveit where they remained until 24 February 1943, when they were placed on a train and sent to Auschwitz concentration camp in Poland. What happened to them is unclear, but it is almost certain that they met their deaths in the camp's notorious gas chambers.

Nasjonal Samling

The Nasjonal Samling Party was formed on 13 May 1933, the same year that the Nazi Party began its rise to power in Germany. Its founder was the former Norwegian minister of defence, Vidkun Quisling, and between 1942 and 1945 it was the only official political party which existed in Norway.

Before the outbreak of war, the party had been viewed by many Norwegians as being comparable with Germany's Nazi Party, which was one of the main reasons why, in a political sense, it had achieved very little and did not even have a single member sitting in the Norwegian parliament. Its main tactic was to organise rallies and marches with socialist and communist protestors, which more often than not would end up in violence and frequently resulted in its future events being banned.

One of its major problems came about as a result of the inability of its members to be able to agree on certain issues. It did not even appear to háve a united front on such major issues as anti-Semitism and religion in general. By 1939, it was a party in name only, with little or no credibility in a political sense and certainly one that had no part to play in Norwegian politics. In essence it had managed to isolate itself by its own actions, which were seen by many Norwegians as controversial.

Quisling and his party saw their opportunity to grab political control of the nation when German forces invaded Norway in April 1940. Quisling made a radio broadcast from Oslo, declared himself the new prime minister of Norway and ordered all Norwegian troops and resistance members to lay down their weapons and surrender to the German authorities. Somewhat surprisingly this did not please the German authorities, as it was not what they wanted. They were hoping that Norway's legitimately elected government would remain in power, as anything they subsequently announced would have more credence in the eyes of the Norwegian people. But when it became obvious that the Norwegian government was not going to surrender, the Germans changed tactics and decided that despite it not being their preferred choice, they would officially recognise Quisling as head of a 'puppet' government. For Hitler and the Nazis, it was more a case of being their only real option.

For some peculiar reason, the Germans appeared to be under the misapprehension that they were in a position to demand from King Haakon that he formally appoint Quisling as the Norwegian prime minister and then return his legitimately appointed government to Oslo. By doing this he would have been effectively and legally sanctioning Germany's invasion of his country. This was a step too far and the king refused.

When the German ambassador to Norway, Curt Bräuer, presented Hitler's demands to Haakon, the king let it be known that he would rather abdicate his throne than ever appoint Quisling, a man whom he personally loathed, as his prime minister. The German reaction to Haakon's less than co-operative response was to bomb the village where they believed the king was staying. They guessed right: the village they bombed was where he had been, but he had left there when the sound of aircraft had been heard overhead. Sadly, he had to stand in the snow in a nearby wood and watch as the village of Nybergsund was destroyed by German bombs.

The Germans realised that Quisling and his party would not be able to muster any significant support from the Norwegian people and quickly washed their hands of him. Instead, on 15 April 1940, an administrative council was established by the Norwegian Supreme Court under the leadership of Ingolf Elster Christensen to administer those areas which had so far come under German control. The council, which held negotiations between Christensen and the Germans, was abolished on 20 September 1940, and although Christensen had been considered as the head of a possible *Riksrad* that could govern Norway, this idea was scrapped when *Reichskommissar* Josef Terboven took over power by forming his own cabinet. Terboven attempted to negotiate an arrangement with the remaining members of the Norwegian parliament that would give a Nazi cabinet the semblance of legitimacy, but these talks failed.

After this, Christensen returned to his office as county governor until 1941, when he was replaced by a member of Quisling's Nasjonal Samling. Enough was enough for Christensen after this; he retired from public life and withdrew to his family farm to see out his days, playing no further part in politics.

With the political situation in Norway almost farcical, the German authorities determined once again to turn to Quisling. On 20 February 1942, nearly two years after they had first invaded the country, they once more made him head of state, although yet again it was Terboven who held the real power, which he was more than happy to prove by conducting numerous counts of political violence whenever it suited him to. Negotiations were all well and good as far as he was concerned – as long as they resulted in him getting his own way. But if he did not, then violence was the ace which he always kept up his sleeve, metaphorically speaking.

Two examples of Terboven's desire to show who really held the power within Norway came in the shape of his imposing martial law in Trondheim, and him ordering the total destruction of the village of Telavag. Whilst Terboven was happily playing 'God' with the lives of ordinary, innocent Norwegians, Quisling seemed to think it was more important to focus on other matters, such as 'economic stability' and 'mediating' between the Norwegian people and the uninvited German occupiers (who were only interested in what they wanted), very little of which brought much in the way of assistance to the people.

An interesting fact about the Nasjonal Samling Party was that its membership did increase slightly over the course of the first few years of the German occupation, but fell off somewhat during 1944 and 1945, the latter of which was possibly connected to the fact that the Norwegians had already worked out for themselves that Germany was clearly losing the war and that it was only a matter of time before it would be over, with the Allied nations coming out on top. Nobody wanted to have been seen to have supported the wrong side, especially if it was against the best interests of their own country, and when it did eventually did come to an end, the last thing any Norwegian wanted to be thought of was a collaborator.

In relation to Trondheim, martial law came into being on 6 October 1942 and lasted for seven days before it finally came to an end on 12 October. Terboven had arrived in Trondheim by train on 5 October, and the following morning he had his soldiers begin posting notices of 'martial law' across the city.

The conditions of martial law imposed by Terboven included a general curfew from 8 pm to 5 am; a prohibition against using railroads and other long distance transportation means; and a prohibition against assembly. Any violations of the curfew were harsh. Penalties for any infringements were punishable with no less than ten years' imprisonment with hard labour, or in extreme cases with capital punishment. To enforce the martial law, Terboven mobilised nearly 13,000 police officers, Hirden and soldiers.

The Hirden was a uniformed paramilitary organisation, formed in 1940 during the German occupation of Norway, and modelled on the German Sturmabteilungen (SA), or 'Brown Shirts'.

In total, about 8,500 Norwegians became members of the Hirden during the war. The organisation was dissolved at the end of the war when Norway was liberated from Nazi rule and many of its former members were arrested, prosecuted and convicted for acts of treason and collaboration with the Nazis. It is quite staggering to think that so many Norwegians so readily turned on their own people.

Members of the Hirden were used to serve as prison-camp guards, but they also regularly worked as a body of men who were empowered to conduct operations against known dissidents, not even having to answer to the police for their actions.

On 6 October 1942, when martial law was declared by Terboven, he also stopped the publication of all Norwegian newspapers.

The German authorities, or rather Terboven, used the period of martial law to murder thirty-four Norwegian civilians, in a case of what the Germans officially referred to as 'extrajudicial execution'. This was the killing of a person, or persons, by governmental authorities or individuals without the sanction of any judicial proceedings or legal process. Such killings often targeted leading political activists, trade union members, dissidents, religious, and social figures, where the German authorities acted as judge, jury and executioner.

Terboven also used the period of martial law to begin the arrest and detention of all Jewish males living in and around the Trondheim area.

In 1942 there were officially known to be at least 2,173 Jews living and working in Norway. The period of martial law saw the beginning of the arrest and detention of some 775 of them, many of whom were deported to concentration camps in Germany. More than half of the Norwegians who died in these camps were Jews. A total of 742 Jews were murdered during their incarceration, and 23 Jews died as a result of extrajudicial execution, murder and suicide during the war, bringing the total of Jewish Norwegian deaths to at least 765. To put this into even further context, this number comprised 230 households. During the Second World War, nearly two-thirds of the Jewish population in Norway fled the country through fear of what would happen to them.

Why martial law was brought in by Terboven, is the obvious question that needs addressing. It was brought in for two reasons. Firstly, there had been a number of acts of sabotage carried out by the Norwegian resistance, which caused the local German authorities a great deal of 'unnecessary extra work' in trying to identify those responsible, and dealing with the aftermath of the individual acts of sabotage. But it was the shooting of two German police officers at Majavatin on 6 September 1942 that pushed Terboven into bringing in martial law. This was also around the same time that Germany was suffering the worst at the Battle of Stalingrad. News of this situation found its way back to the ears of the resistance movement in Norway. There is a suggestion that with this in mind, the imposition of martial law was more to do with the German authorities in Norway sending out a strong message, that they were still a force to be reckoned with, and to prevent the resistance movement from believing they could carry out acts of sabotage with impunity.

Trondheim wasn't the first place where the Germans had employed the use of martial law. They had taken similar action the year before in Oslo.

Terboven certainly played the part of the 'bad guy' to its fullest degree. He thrived on the power which his position gave him. One of the comments that is always raised historically is 'how could anybody do such things?' It is quite simple really. When the only rules in place are the ones that you make; when there is nobody for you to answer to and to tell you to stop; when there are no consequences for you to face for the actions that you have carried out – that is when individuals can, and do such terrible things.

On the evening of the first day of martial law, Terboven drew a large crowd in Trondheim's main square and announced over a loudspeaker that ten local prominent residents had been executed. To try and justify the murders he distastefully used the phrase, 'atonement sacrifices'. They had taken place at 6 pm near the Falstad concentration camp, which was situated to the north of the city of Trondheim. To add insult to injury, he also announced that all of those executed had been stripped of all their financial assets. Terboven used the word confiscated, but he meant 'stolen'.

The ten who were executed were: Trondheim attorney Otto Skirstad; theatre director Henry Gleditsch; newspaper editor Harold Lanqhelle; merchant Hirsch Komissar; engineer Hans Konrad Ekornes; bank president Gunnar Sandberg Birch; Captain Finn Berg; ship owner Per Tangen Lykke; attorney Bull Aakran from Roros; and construction leader Peder Eggen.

What was very perverse about Terboven's announcement was that eight of those he named were actually still alive in a nearby Gestapo headquarters, not that far from the square. Maybe the use of the loud speaker was to ensure that they could hear the announcement of their own deaths. Their murders were, however, later carried out where he said they had been, by firing squad.

That was not the end of the murders during the period of martial law. A further fifteen individuals were shot on 8 October, followed by another nine the next day.

The other twenty-four who were executed were: Peder Stor-Tjonnli, from Majavatn; Johan Audun, Bogfjellmo; Johan Oygard, Aursletta; Einar Oygard, Aursletta; Ole Sæter, Aursletta; Olaf Svebakk, Svebakk; Alf Stormo, Trofors; Oddvar Olsen Majavatn; Magnus Lien Stavasdalen; Edvard Sæter, Sæter; Peter Lund, Saeter; Arne Holmen, Holmen; Mikael Holmen, Holmen; Aksel Johansen, Osterfjorden; Ingvald Melingen, Majavatn; Tormod Tverland, Tverland; Leif Sjofors, Holmen; Bjarne Lien, Stavassdalen; Nils Mollersen, Stavassdalen; Arne Moen, Majavatn; Agnar Blafjellmo, Blafjellmo; Emil Oylund, Majavatn; Peder Forbergskog, Majavatn; and Rasmus Skerpe. (This information is taken from an Internet article 'Martial Law In Trondheim in 1942: Extrajudicial Executions'.)

During the period of martial law, Terboven had his men raid a total of 1,434 homes and arrested a total of 93 individuals. On 12 October, when he deemed that law and order had been re-established to his liking, martial law was lifted.

The reality was quite different. In essence Norway had been under martial law since the beginning of the German occupation and remained so throughout the war. There was no freedom of the press or expression; freedom of assembly was severely curtailed; Norwegians were not free to move around as they chose; the courts had become politicised; all central institutions, ranging from the Church of Norway, teachers' unions, and even athletic events, were compromised in some way by the German authorities or the Nasjonal Samling Party. Terboven's additional implementation of martial law was nothing more than a personal power trip, because there was no one to prevent him from doing otherwise. It was his warped and sadistic way of making a point of letting the Norwegian people know that he was in charge and control of them, and that they lived or died on his whim alone.

The following months in Norway did not get any easier. Many of the country's Jews had been rounded up and sent to Auschwitz, where a number of them would be murdered in the gas chambers.

Thankfully, some of them managed to escape to Sweden, where they hid out until the end of the war.

There was also an increase in the number of what were known as *Nacht und Nebel* incidents, which in English means 'night and fog'.

Nacht und Nebel was a directive which had been issued by Adolf Hitler on 7 December 1941. Its purpose was to target and arrest political activists and resistance fighters. But the effect that it had on the victims' families and the general population was even greater still. The uncertainty as to the fate or whereabouts of these poor unfortunate individuals spread fear in the hearts of everybody. The victims who disappeared in these *Nacht und Nebel* actions were never heard from again.

Until Hitler's directive, prisoners across German-occupied Europe were dealt with the same way they would had have been in most other countries, and certainly within accordance of international agreements and in keeping with the principles of the Geneva Conference. Hitler and his cronies were not great fans of doing things by the rules, unless it suited them to do so of course. They found such rules and regulations to be restrictive and unnecessary, but in deciding to do away with them, they removed, intentionally or otherwise, every traditional and time-honoured restraint on warfare that had ever been in place. This was one of the reasons why such people as Terboven thrived on what they did, because it allowed them to conduct themselves without any restraints. They had total freedom of their actions.

The same day as Hitler's directive, Heinrich Himmler issued the following instructions to the Gestapo.

> After lengthy consideration, it is the will of the Führer that the measures taken against those who are guilty of offences against the Reich or against the occupation forces in occupied areas should be altered. The Führer is of the opinion that in such cases penal servitude or even a hard labour sentence for life will be regarded as a sign

of weakness. An effective and lasting deterrent can be achieved only by the death penalty or by taking measures which will leave the family and the population uncertain as to the fate of the offender. Deportation to Germany serves this purpose.

On 12 December, Field Marshal Wilhelm Keitel of the German Armed Forces High Command issued a directive which further explained Hitler's orders.

Efficient and enduring intimidation can only be achieved either by capital punishment or by measures by which the relatives of the criminals do not know the fate of the criminal.

Keitel was also the man responsible for expanding *Nacht und Nebel* into all countries that were occupied by the military forces of Nazi Germany throughout Europe. If the original directive from Hitler was not sinister enough, Keitel made it even more daunting by expanding on it. In February 1942, he wrote a letter to his commanders informing them that any prisoners who had not been executed within eight days of their capture were to be handed over to the Gestapo so that they could be secretly sent to Germany for further interrogation. Such measures, he said, would have a deterrent effect on others because these individuals would, to all intents and purposes, simply vanish without a trace, and the German authorities would provide no information concerning their whereabouts or what had happened to them.

Keitel's rationale behind his instruction was that it would intimidate local populations, including the friends and families of these prisoners. In essence it was a form of military control by German occupation forces in Norway. Fear of the unknown is and always has been an extremely powerful medium.

To this day, it is not known or been confirmed how many individuals were spirited away by German authorities as a result of this directive. Nothing is known of their fate, which for their families meant not knowing when, where or how they met their deaths.

The *Nacht und Nebel* programme was commented on at the post-war Nuremberg trials, where it was decided that the untold number of disappearances committed under the umbrella of the programme were classed as war crimes. Those individuals who disappeared were predominantly from countries such as Norway. Their arrests were usually carried out during the dead of night, with them immediately being taken to a prison that might be hundreds of miles away from where they lived, where they were interrogated before eventually being sent to a camp to be 'disposed of'. Three main concentration camps were used for these unfortunate individuals; Natzweiler-Struthof was the main one, but similar camps were also used at Esterwegen and Gross-Rosen.

Up to and including 30 April 1944, a total of 6,639 people were known to have been arrested and disappeared, never to be seen again, as a result of the *Nacht und Nebel* programme, including individuals from Norway.

The Hitler directive that was issued on 7 December 1941, and which included the following points, feels somewhat strange when taking into account the countries in which it was used were, at the time, occupied by an unwanted aggressor in the shape of Nazi Germany. Why they were subsequently so surprised at the reactions displayed by these sovereign nations, including elements who did not appreciate their presence, I am at a loss to fully comprehend.

> Within the occupied territories, communistic elements and other circles hostile to Germany have increased their efforts against the German State and the occupying powers since the Russian campaign started. The amount and the danger of these machinations oblige us to take

severe measures as a deterrent. First of all the following directives are to be applied:

I. Within the occupied territories, the adequate punishment for offences committed against the German State or the occupying power which endanger their security or a state of readiness is on principle the death penalty.

II. The offences listed in paragraph I as a rule are to be dealt with in the occupied countries only if it is probable that sentence of death will be passed upon the offender, at least the principal offender, and if the trial and the execution can be completed in a very short time. Otherwise the offenders, at least the principal offenders, are to be taken to Germany.

III. Prisoners taken to Germany are subject to military procedure only if particular military interests require this. In case German or foreign authorities inquire about such prisoners, they are to be told that they have been arrested but that the proceedings do not allow any further information.

IV. The Commanders in the occupied territories and the Court authorities within the framework of their jurisdiction are personally responsible for the observance of this decree.

V. The Chief of the High Command of the Armed Forces determines in which occupied territories this decree is to be applied. He is authorized to explain and to issue executive orders and supplements. The Reich Minister of Justice will issue executive orders within his own jurisdiction.

In using such a programme, Nazi Germany made it much more difficult for the governments of other countries, or humanitarian organisations such as the Red Cross, to accuse the German authorities of any specific misconduct because it had hidden the truth as to whether or not any or all of those who had been arrested as part of *Nacht und Nebel* had been imprisoned or murdered, let alone the cause of the person's disappearance. Because of this uncertainty, the Nazis could not be held accountable. This meant that Nazi Germany was able to abuse, ignore and disregard any and all international treaties and conventions which it chose to. It was not possible to hold them to account for the treatment of certain individuals if it could not be ascertained where a victim was, or what had happened to them.

The other aspect of this situation was that by keeping the truth of what they were doing from the public at large, there was less chance of their own people turning against them.

On 26 April 1942, a number of Gestapo officers arrived in the Norwegian village of Telavåg as they had received information that two members of the Norwegian Independent Company 1, more commonly referred to as the Linge Company or Kompani Linge after their commander, Captain Martin Jensen Linge, Distinguished Service Cross (DSC). The company had been formed in March 1941 to carry out operations on behalf of the SOE. Its members included many talented individuals who carried out numerous operations against their German occupiers, throughout Norway.

The two men in question were Arne Meidal Værum and Emil Gustav Hvaal. But there was no way either of the men were going to surrender, even if it meant losing their own lives. There was an exchange of gunfire which resulted in the deaths of two of the Gestapo officers, Gerhard Berns and Henry Bertram, along with Arne Værum. As for Emil Hvaal, he was captured and, along with his son, was executed a few months later.

The death of two of Josef Terboven's men provided him with the opportunity to indulge in one of his favourite pastimes: killing people. Four days later, Terboven and a large number of German soldiers arrived in Telavåg, a coastal fishing village, to exact their revenge. Every building in the village was destroyed. The villagers' boats were either confiscated along with all of their livestock or sunk. But the reprisals did not stop there. A number of men were executed in the village, with more than seventy others deported and sent to the Nazi concentration camp at Sachsenhausen in north-east Germany. Of these men, thirty-one were murdered whilst prisoners at the camp.

The village's women and children were taken away and kept in custody for some two years. But still this was not enough for Terboven. Along with some of his men he went to the internment camp at Trandum, selected eighteen of the Norwegian prisoners being held there, and had them shot. It is worth noting that at the end of the war, a total of 194 bodies were discovered in a mass grave in Trandum woods. This included 173 who were identified as being Norwegian, 6 who were British civilians and 15 who were Russian civilians.

In response to the manoeuvrings of Quisling and the Germans, King Haakon announced that Norway already had a legitimately elected prime minister and a government, who were with him in London, and that he did not recognise or support anything that Quisling and his party were attempting to do. The Norwegian government in exile announced that resistance to German occupation was to continue.

The response of King Haakon and his government lost Quisling and his party much of their popularity amongst the Norwegian people, which made them of little use to the occupying German authorities. But despite this, their membership grew steadily from just a few hundred to more than 43,000 by November 1943.

Early on in the German occupation, Josef Terboven appointed a 'puppet' government made up of Quisling and other members of the Nasjonal Samling Party. Terboven did however allow them an element of autonomy, but only in relation to civilian matters.

The aftermath of war is usually when the recriminations take place, and it is always the vanquished who suffer. For those who were in charge of the defeated nations, the consequences were, more often than not, much more severe than that of the common soldier, and this is most definitely compounded when collaboration is involved.

In Norway after the war, the authorities prosecuted every known member of the Nasjonal Samling Party, which in 1945 numbered some 50,000. Of these, nearly half were sent to prison, but for Quisling, some of the party's other high-ranking members, along with a few prominent Nazi officials, the consequences for their wartime actions were a lot more severe: for them it was the death penalty.

After the war, Quisling was put on trial for embezzlement, murder and high treason. He was found guilty of all charges, sentenced to death, and executed by firing squad in Oslo on 24 October 1945.

Although from a moral perspective there would be few Norwegians who would have had a problem with their government's actions in how they dealt with Quisling and the others, their actions did raise certain legal points from a Norwegian point of view. This included the fact that Norway did not have capital punishment as part of its legal framework in peacetime, when Quisling and his colleagues were executed, which meant technically there would be a solid argument for suggesting that those sentences could and should not have been carried out. Another similar issue was that at the time the Norwegian constitution only allowed for the use of capital punishment for war crimes whilst the war was taking place, not after it had finished.

Although Norway was occupied by Germany between 1940 and 1945, and Germany had declared war on her on 9 April 1940, Norway had never declared war on Germany.

In relation to the Bredtveit concentration camp, in 1945 the Norwegian authorities turned it into a women's prison for those females awaiting trial for having collaborated with German soldiers during the occupation. In nearly all cases this related to personal relationships.

Before the war had even begun, Germany offered Norway, along with other Scandinavian countries, the opportunity to sign non-aggression pacts with her, which guaranteed their neutrality in the case of a subsequent war. The three nations of Sweden, Norway and Finland, rejected the offer, as they felt by doing so would directly affect their neutrality.

It was a complex time for Norway because it was important for her government to keep its neutrality, as it had done during the First World War, but it became increasingly difficult for her. It was problematic because she had in place trade treaties with both Germany and Great Britain, who in turn both saw strategic advantages in being able to befriend and influence Norway in what she was prepared to allow the other side to do.

What has become known as the Altmark incident, which took place off Jossingfjord, and in Norwegian waters, highlighted just how difficult trying to stay neutral could be.

During 16 and 17 February 1940, a German merchant tanker, the *Altmark*, was sailing through Norwegian waters on its way back to Germany. Its 'cargo' was some 300 British merchant seamen, whose ships had been sunk by the German battleship, the *Graf Spee*. Whilst in Norwegian coastal waters the *Altmark* was, at the request of the British authorities, stopped and boarded on three separate occasions by vessels of the Royal Norwegian Navy. Each time the Norwegian boarding party inexplicably failed to search the ship's cargo hold, and also failed to hear the banging of the British prisoners being held inside, and the *Altmark* was allowed to continue on her way. The problem for the ship's German crew and the Norwegian authorities, was that British authorities already knew that there were British merchant seamen on board the *Altmark*, hence why they had wanted the Norwegians to intercept it in their native waters.

Following the third boarding, *Altmark* was escorted southwards by three vessels from the Royal Norwegian Navy: The *Skary,* the *Kjell* and the *Firem*. Later the same day, aircraft from the Royal Air Force spotted the *Altmark,* at which time it was still off the Norwegian coast. Having realised she had been spotted from the air, she sailed for cover into the Jossingfjord, which is some 2 miles long and 2½ miles wide and surrounded by steep mountains. But the British were not to be put off, and HMS *Cossack* of the Royal Navy, who was quickly on scene, followed the *Altmark* into Jossingfjord.

As the *Cossack* approached the *Altmark*, to her surprise, not only did the three escorting Norwegian vessels not move out of the way, but they pointed their torpedo tubes at the *Cossack*. Uncertain how to respond to what could only be described as unwarranted provocation, the *Cossack*'s Captain Philip Vian, contacted the Admiralty in London, requesting orders on how best to handle the situation.

> Unless Norwegian torpedo-boat undertakes to convoy *Altmark* to Bergen with a joint Anglo-Norwegian guard on board, and a joint escort, you should board *Altmark*, liberate the prisoners, and take possession of the ship pending further instructions. If Norwegian torpedo-boat interferes, you should warn her to stand off. If she fires upon you, you should not reply unless attack is serious, in which case you should defend yourself, using no more force than is necessary, and ceasing fire when she desists. Suggest to Norwegian destroyer that honour is served by submitting to superior force.

The Norwegian escort vessels who had prevented the *Cossack* from approaching the *Altmark* were informed by Captain Vian of what he had been instructed to do.

The Norwegians refused to take part in such a joint escort, and instead repeated their earlier assertions that their earlier searches of *Altmark* had found nothing untoward. Vian then informed the Norwegian officers in charge that he intended to board *Altmark* to conduct a search of the vessel and invited the Norwegians to be present when he and his men did so, but this offer was declined.

Whilst still in the fjord, and in an attempt at preventing Vian and his men from boarding her, the *Altmark* ran aground. The British then went ahead as planned and boarded her at 10 pm on 16 February, and were immediately met with armed resistance by the German sailors. This led to some close-quarter, hand-to-hand combat with the use of bayonets. After eventually defeating the German sailors on board the *Altmark*, Vian and his men went down to the ship's hold. There they discovered the British merchant seamen huddled together in less than convivial conditions.

One of the released prisoners stated that the first they knew of the operation was when they heard the shout 'any Englishmen here?' from the boarding party. When the prisoners shouted back 'yes! We are all British!' the response was 'well, the navy's here!' which brought a response of loud cheers.

Because of the crew's aggressive response to being boarded, a total of eighteen of their number were killed during the rescue mission, one which the German authorities saw differently. To them it was a breach of international law and a violation of Norway's neutrality. Somewhat surprisingly in the circumstances, the British government did not make any objection to the fact that the *Altmark* had taken her 'cargo' of prisoners of war through Norway's neutral waters, but then maybe there was a reason for that silence. But what was odd about the *Altmark* being in Norway's waters in the first place, was that she had travelled hundreds of miles out of her way to get there, with no real explanation as to why.

Norwegian authorities had not given permission for the transportation of prisoners of war through their waters. The *Altmark* was not showing on her manifesto as carrying any, neither had her crew been honest about the nature of their cargo and voyage. But despite this, the only ones in breach of international maritime law was Britain, by carrying out what was after all a military action, in waters of a neutral country, because the passage of prisoners of war through neutral waters was not forbidden by international law.

It was an interesting incident in more ways than one. Norway was far from happy with what transpired, and was said to have been particularly annoyed about her neutrality having been infringed, a comment which had to have been aimed at the part Britain played, because as we already know, three Norwegian naval vessels were escorting the *Altmark* as it sailed through her waters. Either a country declares herself neutral, or she does not, but any country who declares herself as being neutral should not act as the Norwegians did in escorting a German vessel through her waters.

After the *Altmark* incident there was uncertainty on all sides. At the beginning of the war, Norway had declared herself as neutral, but was left feeling concerned about that status. She was right to think along those lines, as the incident had left both Britain and Germany with their own doubts as to the level of her neutrality. The bigger concern was if Norway moved away from being a neutral state, whose side she would come down on?

What was not necessarily known at that time was the *Altmark* incident, and the subsequent uncertainty it had caused, was in essence responsible for Hitler's decision to invade and occupy Norway. The real issue was actually Sweden, from where Germany obtained her iron ore. Hitler was left believing that if Britain acted in relation to Norway then he could lose his vital supply of iron ore, because whichever side either controlled Norway or had her as her as an ally, ultimately dictated whether the much-needed iron ore from Sweden could be transported through Norwegian waters and on to Germany.

With this in mind, Hitler ordered a plan to be drawn up for the invasion of both Norway and Denmark, code named Operation Weserübung. Hitler's desire to invade both countries was not an intention or need to increase the size of the lands that he occupied, it was more about ensuring that Britain did not get her hands on Sweden's iron ore, much needed for the production of steel and understandably in very high demand throughout the war. Germany in particular had already lost other similar sources due to sea blockades carried out by the Royal Navy during the Battle of the Atlantic.

In the early months of the war, Winston Churchill was the First Lord of the Admiralty, and Swedish iron ore was still being sold to Germany so that she could continue fighting the war. Churchill certainly had his finger on the pulse of what was going on and what needed to be done to prevent Germany from gaining any advantages. He spent a lot of time trying to persuade his cabinet colleagues to send a Royal Navy fleet into the Baltic Sea, to prevent ships filled with iron ore from Sweden reaching Germany. Eventually Churchill's pleas were listened to, but it was to be a slow-moving operation. The Admiral of the Fleet, William Boyle, the 12th Earl of Cork, was put in charge of the planning of Operation Catherine.

Churchill's proposal called for a large Royal Navy squadron to include three Revenge-Class battleships, an aircraft carrier, five cruisers, two destroyers, an unspecified number of submarines, and supporting auxiliaries. Some of the vessels would need modifying due to the perceived methods of how they might be attacked and the shallow waters they would mainly be sailing through.

It was also hoped that besides physically stopping iron ore from reaching Germany, the show of strength that such a fleet would deliver would also encourage all the Scandinavian countries to join the Allies in their fight against Nazi Germany.

But before Churchill's idea could get anywhere near impressing and convincing the Scandinavians into siding with the Allies, he had to get it approved and agreed on by the British government and senior military personnel.

Not everybody was in agreement with Churchill's plan, for a number of reasons. One of those who was against the idea was the First Sea Lord, Admiral Sir Dudley Pound. He reminded Churchill that the large quantity of plate armour, which would be needed by the vessels in the proposed fleet, was in short supply and what was available was more urgently needed in other theatres of war. Remembering of course that at the time Italy and Japan, although teetering on the brink, had not yet entered the war. There was also concern what the knock-on effect morale-wise might be if the squadron of aircraft required in Churchill's plan were destroyed or put out of action. There was also the concern on how such a loss might be viewed by both the Japanese and Italians and whether it might influence their decision about entering the war.

Having listened to his dissenters and taken everything into account, including his own views on the matter, Churchill shelved the idea on 20 January 1940. But this setback did not prevent Churchill from trying to do something about Norway. Soon after this, because of the severe wintery conditions, all of the Baltic ports were frozen over, making sailing to and from any of them nigh on impossible. But Germany still needed her iron ore, so had it all delivered by train directly from Sweden to the Norwegian port of Narvik. This in turn led to Churchill pushing the Royal Navy to lay mines along the west coast of Norway in an effort to stop German cargo vessels travelling too close to land in Norwegian territorial waters to avoid being intercepted by Royal Navy vessels conducting contraband patrols.

Britain was also applying pressure on the Norwegians for her to use her massive number of merchant vessels to convey, at what might be called a 'competitive rate', British goods to Norway. As if this was not enough for her government to have to contend with,

Britain also wanted her to join the trade embargo she and other Allied nations had in place against Germany, despite the fact that Norway was a neutral country.

Throughout March and April 1940, the British government put in place plans for an invasion of Norway, fearing ever more what German intentions were towards her. The main purpose of any such invasion from Britain's perspective was to be able to reach Sweden's iron ore mines in Gallivare. There was the added bonus with such a plan of invading Norway, that it would divert large numbers of German forces away from France, which would hopefully make life easier for the British Expeditionary Force.

Winston Churchill knew the importance of Narvik to the Germans and the part it played in the movement of iron ore from Sweden to Germany. The problem for Churchill and the British government came when Germany activated its own blitzkrieg-style invasion of Norway, as part of Operation Weserübung on 9 April 1940, by sending aircraft and ten of their destroyers to Narvik. Each of the vessels were carrying 200 mountain-trained infantry troops.

The German destroyers were met by two Norwegian coastal defence vessels, but they were quickly accounted for by the clinical proficiency of the Germans' better-equipped destroyers, and the 2,000 German troops were landed at Narvik.

The Royal Navy missed a great opportunity to confront their German counterparts because of a major storm in the region on 7 April 1940, which somehow contrived to make sure that each side did not see each other in the turbulent waters off the Norwegian coastline.

When German troops tried to land at Oslo, they did not quite have things their own way. The German taskforce, led by their flagship, the *Blucher*, entered the Oslofjord to be met by Norwegian artillery and torpedoes, sinking the *Blucher* in the process and killing some 1,000 soldiers and crew. This delay in the Germans coming ashore was sufficient time for the Norwegian king and his government to escape from the city. All the other ships in the German taskforce were either sunk or destroyed by the Norwegian defences.

The king's escape from Oslo was, thankfully for the Norwegians, timed to perfection, as a German parachute battalion secured the airfields at both Oslo and Stavanger early on in the attack.

Thankfully for the Germans, in the other cities they attacked, Bergen, Kristiansand, Stavanger and Trondheim, they were not met by any real kind of resistance, certainly not anything like what they came up against in Oslo. The operation also included 800 aircraft from the German Luftwaffe, which in effect ensured a swift victory. But what swung it for the Germans, was despite the fact that the Norwegian defenders produced an effective resistance to German seaborne forces, once their airborne troops, who had landed at the nearby airport, triumphantly marched into the city from the rear, the city's defenders only had one real option and that was to surrender.

The British response to discovering that the Germans had already landed in Norway, and had gained a 'foothold', was to expediently send a number of her own ships to Narvik to try and recover the position. Once off the Norwegian coast they engaged and destroyed all the German vessels that had brought the German invasion force to Narvik. This was followed a couple of days later by the arrival of a number of British troops under the command of Major Pierse Joseph Mackesy, but this was where things started to become a bit disjointed. The British admiralty wanted Mackesy to carry out an amphibious assault on Narvik as soon as it was practicable to do so. But Mackesy was reluctant to carry out such an assault, due to a wrongly held belief that the Norwegian coastal defences, now manned by heavily armed and well-trained German soldiers, were too strongly defended for such an attack, and it would all end badly.

The Admiralty in London, somewhat perturbed by Mackesy's response, then suggested a naval bombardment of the Norwegian coastline, focusing on Narvik, which would then allow for the troops to be safely landed immediately after the bombardment had finished. But Mackesy was not happy with this suggestion either, stating that he refused to subject Norwegian citizens to such a bombardment. Instead he landed his men near Narvik where he had them wait until the winter's snow finally melted so that they could finally attack and capture the town.

By the time Narvik had been captured by a combined Norwegian, Polish, French and British force on 28 May 1940, Winston Churchill had become the new British prime minister, and the evacuations at Dunkirk had begun, as the Allies were losing the Battle of France.

As in all wars, difficult decisions have to be made, and theatres of war have to be prioritised. For Britain and her Allies, cutting off Germany's source of iron ore was a priority, because if that could be achieved, it could undoubtedly shorten the war in the long term. In relation to the Battle of France, ensuring the evacuations at Dunkirk were a success was even more of a priority, because if the evacuations at Dunkirk failed and the men (who were subsequently rescued) were captured or killed, then the war was over at that time. This meant that regardless of the pros and cons of the Norway situation, the number one priority for Prime Minister Winston Churchill and his government was undoubtedly the evacuations at Dunkirk.

The interesting aspect about Norway was that it was a case of both countries having the same idea of invading it, with one country, in this case Germany, getting in first. The main reason being the exact opposite to that of Britain and her allies. Germany had to invade Norway to safeguard her iron ore needs from Sweden, and to ensure it had control of the ice-free ports such as Narvik, so that in the winter months she could still ensure the delivery of her iron ore requirements. The Norwegian coastline also provided Germany with a good base from which to operate, whilst also delivering her direct access to the North Sea.

There has always been an amount of criticism levelled at Norway, and certain of her officials, particularly Birger Ljungberg, the minister of defence, and Halvdan Koht, the nation's foreign minister, for being somewhat unprepared for Germany's invasion. This is rather unfair to both men as it would not have mattered how much preparation Norway had made, the outcome would still have been the same, possibly with many more Norwegians killed in the process. Germany's need for the iron ore provided by Sweden would have dictated that she would have done whatever necessary to fulfil that need. Not having the iron ore simply was not an option.

Once the Germans had established a solid base in the cities of Oslo and Trondheim, they launched a ground offensive against Norwegian resistance groups in the area. As an offensive fighting unit, the resistance groups achieved very little in a military sense, but their self-belief, resilience and dogged determination helped provide the time needed to ensure that their king and government officials were not captured by the Germans. If they had been, the outcome for Norway could have been very different to what it eventually was.

Norway was never set up to be a nation on the offensive. Its neutral stance on the war and the manner in which it conducted its business was proof enough of that. Largely due to this it did not own too much in the way of state-of-the-art military equipment, but what it did have was treated with respect. Nearly all of Norway's best military equipment was lost to the Germans within the first twenty-four hours of the invasion.

In essence the Norwegian army was in shock, after all, its men would never have expected to have been in such a situation, as they were a neutral country. The shock of being invaded by Germany must have been an immense one. One can only guess at the confusion and uncertainty caused by the government's initial mobilisation order, but that is not to suggest that these men were anything other than very brave individuals.

Once they had shaken the cobwebs away, dusted themselves down, the Norwegian defenders put up a solid defence, which for a period of time managed to halt the German advance. But it was always going to be only a matter of time before they were overwhelmed. It is more than likely that the Germans were taken back at the ability and determination of the relatively inexperienced Norwegian defenders. In the end it was always going to be the Germans, who were fitter, better trained, battle-hardened and superior in numbers, who would prevail, and once they brought into play their Panzer and machine-gun battalions, it was in effect, 'game over'.

Despite their inexperience, the Norwegian soldiers did not panic or lose their nerve, although it would have been understandable if they had. Instead they thought about the tactics they could employ to provide sufficient time for Britain to send some much-needed reinforcements.

It was to be no easy task for the British, it wasn't as if they could just turn up unannounced and all would be well again. That was never going happen. It was 13 April 1940 before ships of the Royal Navy arrived off the coast of Norway, close to the port of Narvik. There ensued a battle with the German defenders, in the fjord, and by the time the guns on both sides had finally been silenced, the Germans had reportedly lost one submarine and as many as eight destroyers. Despite the British 'victory' there was no rush to storm troops on to the beaches and into the middle of the city. But what was to follow was an intriguing game of 'cat and mouse'. It was the following day before British and French troops started to land at Narvik, but it did not stop there. Soon after the initial landings at Narvik, other British troops landed at Namsos and Andalsnes, to enable them to carry out an attack on the city of Trondheim, from both the north and south. Unbeknown to the British, the Germans had landed troops behind theirs at both Namsos and Andalsnes, leaving them in an extremely precarious position.

The British who were being out-manoeuvred, and who were certainly outnumbered by the Germans, were limited in what to do next. Added to this, their senior commanders would have been fully aware of the worsening position in France, and with that already looking as though it was going to end in defeat, the last thing that the public back home in Britain would want to hear, would be news of yet another substantial defeat at the hands of the Germans.

The reluctant decision to evacuate all British troops from Norway was taken on 26 April 1940, by the British government, on the advice of senior military figures, but it still took a week before the first of the evacuations of British soldiers actually began, with British troops at Namsos and Andalsnes evacuated on 2 May 1940. This did not mark the immediate end for the Norwegian defenders as might have been expected. Instead they fought on and held out until 5 May 1940, when they were finally defeated at Hegra Fortress in central Norway and in the south of the country at Vinjesvingen.

In the north of the country, where there were a large number of British and French troops, it was a totally different situation. In what had become known as the Battle of Narvik, German forces held out against a much larger and combined British and French force, before managing to make their way out of Narvik on 28 May. By now, Winston Churchill had been the British prime minister for just over two weeks, and the evacuations of British and Allied troops were already underway at Dunkirk.

With the events and happenings in France, and the belief that Britain could face an imminent invasion threat herself if it all went wrong for her on the beaches at Dunkirk, the remaining 25,000 British and French troops began leaving Narvik on 3 June 1940, less than two weeks after her successes there.

The bravery of the Norwegians was once again visible for everybody to see, with the remnants of her 6th Division holding out until 10 June 1940 before they finally surrendered, but only after the last of the British and French troops had been safely evacuated. To put the Norwegians' defence of their country into some kind of context, it is worth noting that they held out against the German invaders for some two months before finally surrendering. This was the longest period of time that an invaded country had been able to hold out against the Germans during the course of the war.

Hitler's victory in Norway had proved extremely beneficial for Germany. With some 300,000 of her troops garrisoned in the country throughout the war, it safeguarded her supplies of the much-needed iron ore, without which her ability to sustain a solid and progressive war footing for so long would have been greatly affected. It provided a number of air fields and sea ports for her air force and navy to be able to attack Britain from across the North Sea, and lastly it ensured that the likelihood of a large-scale, sea-borne invasion of Norway was extremely unlikely, which it proved to be.

Throughout the war, the *Oberkommando der Wehrmacht* in Germany was still in command of such military forces as the Heer and the Luftwaffe. The Heer, a not so commonly used title, was the land forces element of the Wehrmacht German army. Other than this, the person in Norway who was in charge of all other military agencies was the Reich Commissioner.

To ensure total political control throughout Norway, all political parties, except one, were banned by the Nazi authorities. The only party allowed was the Nazi-backed Nasjonal Samling Party, and it was through them that the Nazis were able to push through and bring in to being whatever legislation and policies that they saw fit. Even other organisations such as trade unions were forced to appoint as their leaders members of the Nasjonal Samling Party. Although amongst the civilian population there was much in the way of a verbal outpouring of resistance against Nazi-imposed legislation and policies, the reality was that there was little, if anything, they could do to prevent the implementation of such Nazi edicts.

The Norwegian people were more inclined to be less confrontational when it came to Nazi ideas on the topics of ensuring the continuation of economic activity and anything to do with the continuation and social welfare programme.

To ensure that Nazi Germany held on to one of its prized possessions in the shape of Norway, it made the country the most heavily fortified nation in the world with the number of men it had stationed there; at its peak there was one German soldier for every eight Norwegian civilians. From a German soldier's perspective it was a 'plumb' posting, well at least for those who were not 'diehard' Nazis or fanatical members of Hitler's SS units. For those who had been conscripted into the German army and who just wanted to keep their heads down and see out their time until the war was over, a posting to Norway was as good as it could possibly get. A bit of sentry duty maybe, the odd search or two for resistance fighters, and at worst, maybe a few frightening air raids to have to live through. Compared with a posting to France, fighting against the British, or on the Eastern Front in Russia, a posting to Norway was welcome.

During the Second World War, the Schutzstaffel (the SS) had a strength of 6,000 men permanently stationed in Norway, such was the level of Norwegian resistance-related incidents. They came under the command of Obergruppenführer Wilhelm Rediess, who was an interesting character.

At the beginning of the war, he was responsible for the implementation of Nazi Germany's racial laws in Prussia, which meant him overseeing the deportation of Jews from East Prussia to concentration camps in Poland. He was also the man responsible for 'eradicating', or rather murdering, 1,558 Jewish deportees, whom the German authorities had deemed to be mentally ill. To achieve this he took himself to an entirely new level of Nazi extremism. He acquired a number of gas vans, an early method of murdering Jewish civilians. He then gathered a number of SS men, to whom he had promised a bounty of 10 Reichsmark for each Jew killed. The task of disposing of them all in such a gruesome and inhumane manner was eventually achieved, but it took nineteen days before the last of them was killed. Once the task had been completed, Rediess then refused to pay his men the bounty that they had been promised at the outset.

Rediess had been transferred to Norway, after the completion of the German invasion of the country, to work alongside the newly appointed Reichskommissar, Josef Terboven.

During his time in Norway, Rediess came up with a somewhat unusual, yet far-reaching programme, the remnants of which still linger in Norwegian society even today. In early 1941, he was made aware of the large number of Norwegian women who had become pregnant as a result of fraternisation with German soldiers. Rather than becoming angered by such events, he instigated a *Lebensborn* programme throughout Norway, which actively encouraged the conception and birth of racially pure, blond-haired, blue-eyed 'Aryan' children. Most of the fathers in this programme were fanatical SS troops, who were ultimately responsible for the birth of some 8,000 children.

As for Rediess, he eventually showed his true colours. When the war came to an end, and Germany had finally been defeated, rather than surrender and face up to the consequences of his wartime actions, he took the coward's way out and committed suicide by shooting himself in the head with his own pistol. He has no burial plot as his body was lost as a result of the explosion which killed Josef Terboven, when he too committed suicide later the same day (8 May 1945) in the basement of the Skaugum Manor building in Oslo.

With such events taking place across Norway, it is no wonder that many Norwegians wanted to escape the country and make their way to the UK. It would also in part explain why so many Norwegian men either joined the Norwegian resistance movement, or became members of the Shetland Bus programme to do their bit to bring the German occupation of their country to an end at the earliest opportunity.

Although it could be argued that much of this has little to do directly with the Shetland Bus operation, it certainly provides a background to what life was like in Norway during the German occupation, and help explain the desire by many young Norwegian men to become involved with the Shetland Bus programme, and why they were readily prepared to risk their own lives in the process.

In essence, they were prepared to do whatever it took to rid their country of their German oppressors.

The German occupation of Norway had other numerous pronounced effects on the country. Prior to the occupation, Norway had a strong economy with numerous trading partners throughout Europe. Almost immediately after German troops set foot on Norwegian soil, all of that stopped. She lost all of her major trading partners. Her only trading partner after April 1940 was Nazi Germany. But it was not a profitable partnership for Norway, as all Germany did was take by way of confiscation. What Norway had left she needed for her own people. Basic commodities, particularly food, quickly became scarce, and there was a real risk of a famine enveloping the country. To survive, the people had to grow their own crops such as potatoes, tomatoes and a varied range of vegetables, and keep their own animals such as rabbits, chickens and pigs. Fishing by both rod and boat increased dramatically, over and above the normal levels of this long-term seafaring nation.

It also proved a good cover for the Shetland Bus programme, as there were so many fishing vessels leaving towns and villages the length and breadth of the country, that it was impossible for the German authorities to monitor all of the comings and goings. It was this environment which allowed the SOE to be so successful in landing its agents, equipment and supplies at numerous locations up and down the coast of Norway, and safely extracting them, along with hundreds of refugees who were safely brought back to the UK.

As was the case for many European countries, Norway also had a Jewish population at the outbreak of the Second World War, and regardless of the reasons why Germany had invaded Norway, she certainly was not going to ignore dealing with Norwegian Jews, in exactly the same way as she had with every other country she had occupied throughout Europe.

A number of the Jewish population who had managed to escape from German-occupied Norway had done so via the Shetland Bus route across the North Sea.

A distasteful aspect of any occupation of a country by a foreign power, is that of the collaboration of the country's civilian population with the authorities of the occupying nation. Norway was no different.

One of the country's most notorious collaborators was Henry Oliver Rinnan, who was the leader of a group of Norwegian pro-active collaborators and informants who managed to infiltrate elements of the Norwegian resistance movement, resulting in the capture and murder of a number of its members. How many of these were connected in some way to the workings of the Shetland Bus, is unknown.

Other collaborators were those who worked for the Statspolitiet, a police force which worked outside of the confines of the country's regular police, and were answerable to the Sicherheitspolizei or the German Security Police. They also had a strong connection with the Quisling political regime.

In addition to these two groups there was also the Hirden, an armed, fascist, paramilitary group which wore German-style uniforms and helmets and was directly connected to the ruling Quisling party, taking its orders from the Sicherheitspolizei. The members were more than prepared to use violence against their own people if they deemed it necessary to do so.

As if that wasn't enough, a further 15,000 Norwegians willingly signed up to fight for Nazi Germany, 6,000 of whom fought on the Eastern Front as part of the Germanic SS Regiment.

The Germanic SS, or the *Germanische SS*, was the collective name for Nordic SS units; groups of which had been formed in Belgium, Denmark, Holland and Norway. This was because the German authorities believed those nations to be what they considered as, 'racially suitable'. They were mainly allocated security-type roles such as that of guards or sentries, and in support of Reich Main Security Office units such as the Gestapo.

The Nazis believed that the original homeland of the Aryan-Germanic peoples was in Scandinavia, and therefore Nordic and Germanic blood had the same origins and recruits were thought of by Nazi Germany as being part of the wider Germanic family.

This was the main reason why Nazi Germany was more than happy for the formation of Germanic SS units in countries such as Norway.

Himmler considered the Germanic suitability of people from Norway as being *'blutsmassig unerhort wertvolle Krafte',* which in English translates into, 'by blood exceptionally highly qualified people'.

Norwegian men who enlisted in the Germanic SS enjoyed astonishing privileges, including the allowance to fraternise and have sex with German women, not something Nazi Germany would have allowed if they had not believed in Scandinavia being the original homeland of the Aryan-Germanic peoples.

The man in charge of the central command office of the SS Main Office, was the Nazi fanatic, Gottlob Berger, who held the rank of SS-Obergruppenfuhrer und General der Waffen-SS, the equivalent of rank of lieutenant colonel, thought of the Germanic SS as the means by which Nazi Germany could expand the greater German Empire.

Although convicted of war crimes at the subsequent war trials in Nuremberg between 1946 and 1949, he escaped the death penalty, and was sentenced to twenty-five years' imprisonment. He was released after having served just six years.

With so many Norwegians having been enticed and seduced by the Nazi dream, matters were made extremely difficult for the Shetland Bus and the operatives who worked for it, because they simply did not know whom they could trust.

The Milorg, the name of the Norwegian resistance movement, was not some deeply rooted historical name used to help forge and unite the Norwegian people against a common enemy in the form of Nazi Germany. It was simply an abbreviation of the words 'military organisation'. Its work included the gathering of intelligence, sabotage of identified German targets, raids on strategic locations, espionage, the movement of goods, supplies and equipment, and assisting Norwegian civilians escape, mainly through neutral Sweden.

By the end of the war, the Milorg was a force to be reckoned with, numbering some 40,000 armed men in its ranks. Although there were numerous separate resistance groups throughout Norway, they were well organised at a local level as well as in a national sense. Having such a unified command structure helped greatly at the end of the war when the Germans surrendered and power of the country transferred back to Norwegian authorities.

The Milorg consisted of two sections; the first was the *Hiemmefronten*, or those members who worked on the home front, and whose role included sabotage, intelligence gathering, raids and clandestine operations. The second was those members of the Norwegian resistance who worked outside the country, such as in the Merchant Navy or the Royal Norwegian Navy, who had managed to sail many of her ships to Britain before the occupying Germans had been able to get their hands on them; members of the Norwegian air force who had managed to fly their aircraft over to Britain; as well as numerous commando groups who were working with the SOE out of Shetland and mainland Britain.

The home resistance movement was also involved in the distribution of 'illegal' wartime newspapers, including *Friheten*, which was founded in 1941 by the communist wing of the Norwegian resistance movement. It began life as a newssheet and went on to become a newspaper in its own right, with its first issue dated 14 May 1945, just after Germany had surrendered.

Vart Land, which translates into 'our country', was founded at a meeting on 28 September 1944, but its first publication did not appear until 31 August 1945. Initially it was published as a part of the *Morgenbladet* newspaper, but was subsequently published as a stand-alone broadsheet paper.

As an aside, the *Morgenbladet* had an interesting story. Its editor, Olaf Gierlow and the news editor, were arrested by the Germans in 1941, after refusing directives imposed upon them by the German occupation forces. Roly Werner Erichsen, who replaced Olaf Gierlow as editor, found himself in the Grini detention camp in 1943, at which time the newspaper discontinued publication until the end of the war.

Fritt Land, and a trade union-produced paper, *Fri Fagbevegelse*, were others which the Germans were not happy about as they had no control over the content being read by the Norwegian people.

During the course of the war, an estimated 80,000 Norwegians escaped from their country, mainly for either political or military reasons. Many of them made it to the UK, and by the end of the war some 28,000, Norwegian men and women had enlisted in Allied military forces.

Seeing as the king of Norway and the country's government were in exile in Britain, it made sense for its armed forces to follow. More than a dozen warships of the Royal Norwegian Navy, which included 5 aircraft and 500 sailors, made it across the North Sea to Britain in 1940. The number of both men and ships increased throughout the years of the war, and by the end of it, some 650 Norwegian sailors had lost their lives fighting alongside the Royal Navy.

At the start of the war, the Norwegians had two separate air forces, the Royal Norwegian Naval Air Service and the Norwegian Army Air Service, with most of their training carried out in Canada, although these two branches did amalgamate on 10 November 1940 to become the Royal Norwegian Air Force. Under this new guise, they operated four squadrons that fought alongside Allied forces. No. 330 Squadron, which for most of the war operated in and around Iceland, arrived in Scotland in early 1943, with its final destination being RAF Scatsta in Shetland, as of 20 April 1943. No. 331 Squadron, which was part of Fighter Command between 1941 and 1944, took part in the raid on Dieppe and the Normandy landings. They were stationed at North Weald in Essex along with their compatriots of No. 332 Squadron.

No. 333 Squadron was involved in a number of missions, including searching for German submarines, in support of operations along the Norwegian coastline, which involved them landing in German-occupied Norway and collecting agents (and their radio and transmitter sets) who had previously been taken to Norway as part of the Shetland Bus operation. They also dropped Christmas presents to the Norwegian people, and carried search and rescue missions for downed Allied pilots.

Besides the Norwegian squadrons, there were also a number of Norwegian volunteers who served with the Royal Air Force. A total of 228 Norwegian pilots and air crew were killed whilst fighting alongside their allied counterparts.

The Norwegian army in exile never exceeded 4,000 men. One of its units was Kompani Linge (Norwegian Independent Company 1), which served with the SOE and was included in many of the operations carried out by the Shetland Bus.

CHAPTER THREE

The Setting up of the Special Operations Executive

With Winston Churchill as its main supporter, the Special Operations Executive (SOE) had an enormous amount of autonomy, which would not have been available to the three main branches of Britain's military establishment. In essence it was only accountable to itself. That put it in an enviable situation, which was not always appreciated or liked by other agencies.

One of the advantages of being able to work in such an environment was the SOE could employ whomever they wanted to, regardless of what their background was, or how they fitted in to society's normal allowances of what was acceptable and what was not. If somebody had a skill or an ability that they needed, then what their place in society was, or what dark secret they were hiding in their background, mattered not. It could be said that this was an extremely dangerous strategy because individuals with such flaws were less likely to readily conform as the normal man in the street might be. This in turn meant that they were potentially a big security risk, prepared and willing to sell out to the enemy if the price was right. However, there are no such known cases of such an occurrence of an SOE member having done so. It was their maverick approach to life which made them who they were and gave them their individual skill sets.

In the beginning, SOE radio traffic was transmitted via the SIS-controlled radio station at Bletchley Park, in Buckinghamshire, but by 1 June 1942 it had acquired its own transmitting and receiving stations at Grendon Underwood in Buckinghamshire and Poundon, nearby. This gave them the ability to undertake their operations in comparative secrecy, but at the same time it also provided them with a high level of security.

All agents of the SOE were issued with the Fairbairn Sykes fighting knife, which could be hidden in the heel of a shoe or the collar of a coat or a jacket. These same agents were also provided with suicide pills, which were hidden inside coat buttons. An agent who had the ability to take his own life was at an advantage, as the German interrogation of an agent would not have been a nice affair, and once the interrogation was over they would have no doubt been murdered; once captured, few of them were allowed to survive.

Norway was an ideal location for the operatives and agents of the SOE to hone their plethora of skills. With a total of around 13,000 personnel, they were relatively small in number and known in different circles by a variety of nicknames, which included 'The Baker Street Irregulars', a reference to a group of fictional characters who appear in various stories of Sherlock Holmes, as street boys who are employed by Holmes to act as intelligence agents, 'Churchill's Secret Army', and the 'Ministry of Ungentlemanly Warfare'.

Formed on 22 July 1940, on the instruction of Winston Churchill, their role was that of espionage, irregular warfare, especially sabotage and raiding operations, along with special reconnaissance. They were also responsible for the formation and operations of the Shetland Bus. They were placed under the command of Hugh Dalton, who at the time was the minister of economic warfare. Dalton, later Baron Dalton, served in Winston Churchill's wartime coalition government, obtaining his ministerial position after the Dunkirk evacuations were completed in June 1940.

With the outbreak of the Second World War, Neville Chamberlain's position as the nation's prime minister soon became untenable after a number of Conservative MPs felt unable to support him in the political arena, after the Norway Debate, which took place between 7 and 9 May 1940, ended in MPs holding a vote of no confidence, which although won by the government, left them with a drastically reduced majority. Dalton and other senior Labour party members agreed to be part of a coalition government, but only one that did not have Chamberlain as prime minister.

Dalton was a bitter enemy of Chamberlain and had been particularly opposed to his policy of appeasement of Hitler and Nazi Germany; instead he had openly promoted Britain's full scale re-armament in an attempt to deter any military threat posed by direct and deliberate German aggression. Dalton was appointed minister of economic warfare, where he remained until 22 February 1942, when he became the president of the Board of Trade.

The SOE had arguably already been formed before 1940, as it was a merger of three existing British secret departments which had all come in to being shortly before the outbreak of the Second World War. In March 1938, Department EH (the initials of its headquarters at Electra House in Moorgate, London), had been created by the Foreign Office as a propaganda organisation. The man in charge was Sir Campbell Stuart, the Canadian newspaper magnate.

March 1938 also saw the formation of the Secret Intelligence Service, known as MI6. One of its departments, Section D, was initially based at St Ermin's Hotel in Westminster, before it moved to the Metropole Hotel near Trafalgar Square. It was run by Major Lawrence Grand of the Royal Engineers and was tasked with investigating the use of sabotage techniques, propaganda, and any other covert methods which could be employed to weaken an enemy power. In the 'field' their initial efforts were met with failure, when they were unsuccessful in their attempts at mining a gorge on the River Danube known as the Iron Gate. The reason for the operation was to try and prevent vital materials, which were being sent by river from neutral countries who were still happy to do business with her, from reaching Nazi Germany.

Later that same year, an existing research department of the War Office known as GS(R), was expanded and renamed MI(R). Under the leadership of Major J. C. Holland, Royal Engineers, it conducted research into guerrilla warfare. Part of its work also included the production of pamphlets and technical handbooks for guerrilla leaders. The Independent Companies, which were autonomous units set up to conduct sabotage and guerrilla operations in German-occupied Norway, had been formed by the MI(R). They were also responsible for the Auxiliary Units, or groups of commandos who had secretly been put in place across the UK, to provide a professional military option in the event of a German invasion of Britain, which was a real possibility in the first couple of years of the war.

When Winston Churchill became prime minister on 10 May 1940, after the resignation of Neville Chamberlain, he appointed Lord Hankey as the Chancellor of the Duchy of Lancaster. At his boss's behest, by 13 June Hankey had persuaded Section D and MI(R) that their two organisations should be amalgamated. Matters were formalised at a cabinet meeting on 1 July, where it was decided that Hugh Dalton would take political responsibility for the newly formed Special Operations Executive. He recorded in his diary for 22 July 1940 that Churchill had said to him: 'And now go and set Europe ablaze'.

This new beginning was also the end for Sir Campbell Stuart, who decided to leave the SOE, whilst both majors Grand and Holland returned to their regiment, the Royal Engineers, to take up other positions. In came Foreign Office civil servant Gladwyn Jebb, who became the organisation's chief executive officer, and Brigadier Colin Gubbins, who became director of operations.

Another department, which Winston Churchill gave his enthusiastic support to and showed a close interest in, was MIR(c), which was responsible for the development of weapons for use in the arena of irregular warfare. It was an independent organisation, run by Major Millis Jefferis, MC, and which never formally became part of the SOE. It was a department of the Ministry of Defence, in fact the only unit of the Ministry. It was also known as MD1 and was located at a country house named 'The Firs' in Whitchurch, Buckinghamshire. The organisation acquired the nickname of 'Churchill's Toyshop'.

In 1940, Major Jefferis was sent to Norway and on his return he gave a personnel account of his activities to Winston Churchill, who briefed his War Cabinet with what Jefferis had told him, the content of that meeting recorded thus:

> The Prime Minister gave the War Cabinet an account of the report which had been made personally to him by Major Jefferis. Major Jefferis had been sent to Andalsnes with instructions to blow up the Western Railway in Central Norway. He had accordingly gone down the railway line and joined Brigadier Morgan's Brigade; but the Norwegians had categorically refused to allow him to carry out any demolitions. He had been present when Morgan's Brigade had been engaged by the enemy. The Germans had attacked with artillery, tanks and armoured cars, which our troops had been without. Far more destructive of morale, however, had been the low flying attacks with bombs and machine guns. Although the casualties had not been so great as from shell fire, the moral effect of seeing the aircraft coming, of being unable to take cover, of being able to observe the bomb dropping, and of the terrific explosion, had been overwhelming.
>
> Jefferis had eventually found himself with the Germans behind him. Picking up a sergeant and two privates, he had succeeded in making his way back to Andalsnes; and on the way he had managed to blow up the girders of two bridges on the German side. He estimated that it would take some three weeks to repair these. At Andalsnes the

conditions of air attack had been such as to make it quite impossible to walk down to the jetty during the daylight hours. He had spent a day in a sloop in the harbour at which thirty bombs had been aimed. None had hit, but the immunity of a ship under such conditions could only be, in Major Jefferis's opinion, a matter of time, and he calculated that his life would probably not be more than three days.

The general conclusion which he (the prime minister) drew from Major Jefferis's account was that it was quite impossible for land forces to withstand complete air superiority of the kind which the Germans had enjoyed in Norway. This made it all the more imperative to the success of our operations at Narvik that we should establish air bases in that area, not only for fighters, but also for bombers.

Major Jefferis was Mentioned in Despatches for his efforts in Norway, as well as being awarded the Norwegian Cross with sword, the announcement of which was made in the *London Gazette* on Tuesday, 11 August 1942.

During the course of the Second World War, MD1 was responsible for the introduction into military service of twenty-six different types of devices, including the Sticky Bomb, a hand-held anti-tank weapon, the Projector, Infantry, Anti Tank (PIAT), portable anti-tank weapon, and a magnetic Limet naval mine.

Jefferis was liked and respected by Winston Churchill to such a degree that after he lost his position as prime minister in the general election of 1945, Churchill promoted Jefferis from Commander of the Order of the British Empire, (CBE) to Knight Commander of the British Empire (KBE) in his resignation honours list.

Notable leaders of the SOE included Frank Nelson. At the beginning of the Second World War he was the Consul to Basel in

Switzerland, but when Germany invaded France in 1940, he was driven by Richard Arnold-Baker to the mouth of the Gironde river where a British Steam Ship, the *Nariva,* picked them up and took them back to London so that Nelson could become the first chief of the SOE, a position to which he was appointed by the War Office. Nelson worked so hard in his new role that he was diagnosed as suffering with exhaustion. This affected his health so badly that he had to retire from his position in 1942.

Charles Jocelyn Hambro had a long-standing military background, having served during the First World War. He passed out of Sandhurst Military College as an ensign in the Coldstream Guards on 22 December 1915, and was immediately posted to the Western Front, where he served for two years until he was demobbed. He was promoted to the rank of lieutenant on 10 July 1916, and awarded the Military Cross (MC) on 26 September 1917 for conspicuous bravery in action. The citation for his award, which appeared in the *London Gazette,* reads as follows:

> For conspicuous gallantry and devotion to duty. Accompanied by a private, he crossed to the enemy's side of a canal and rescued two wounded men, one of whom was unable to walk, from close under the enemy's parapet. Later in the day, he went forward in charge of the leading patrol of an advance, personally accounting for four of the enemy with his revolver and capturing several prisoners with his party. On reaching his objective, he sent back correct and valuable information, and has at all times displayed the utmost coolness and gallantry.

A man with a military pedigree it might be said.

During the inter-war years he worked in banking, initially in his family run bank, J.C. Hambro, then after its amalgamation with the British Bank of Northern Commerce, when it became Hambro's

Bank. In 1928, he was also made a director of the Bank of England, at the relatively young age of 30.

When the Second World War began, he was asked by Ronald Cross, the minister of economic warfare between 1939 and 1940, to join his department, which in essence was a cover name and organisation for the SOE. Hambro accepted the offer, and was placed in charge of its Scandinavian operations. Wealthy in his own right, but a relatively humble man, Hambro refused to take any wages for wartime military work with the SOE.

Hambro most definitely had a heavy work load to contend with, which was added to between December 1940 and November 1941, as he was also in charge of the Belgian, Dutch, French and German sections of the SOE. In 1942, he succeeded Frank Nelson as the man in overall charge of the SOE. One of his first major actions in his new role, was to meet with his opposite number in charge of the American Office of Strategic Services (which went on to become the Central Intelligence Agency), Colonel William Joseph 'Wild Bill' Donovan.

Hambro resigned his position as head of the SOE in 1943. For the rest of the war he was in charge of the British Raw Materials Mission in Washington, a cover organisation which had been put in place simply to allow Britain and America to exchange information and technology. This eventually led to the detonation of the first atomic bomb, as part of what was named the Manhattan Project.

Brigadier Colin Gubbins became the Chief of Staff of the military mission in Poland when he arrived in Warsaw on 3 September 1939, within just a matter of hours of war having been declared by Britain on Hitler's Nazi Germany. But circumstances changed so quickly as German forces smashed their way into Poland that within a matter of days, Gubbins and the rest of the mission's staff had to leave Warsaw or risk being captured and spending the rest of the war in a prisoner of war camp. By the end of September, all the mission's members had safely made it out of Poland and into neighbouring Romania.

What had impressed Gubbins and the head of the British Military Mission to Poland, Adrian Carton de Wiart, VC, was the speed and effectiveness of the German Panzer tank tactics. They made good their escape to Romania together with the Polish commander Edward Rydz-Śmigły, with both German and Soviet forces in hot pursuit. But it was not long before matters deteriorated in Romania, and Gubbins, Carton de Wiart, and the rest of the British Military Mission had to escape from there, which they did by aircraft on 21 September 1939, using false passports. The very same day, the pro-Allied Romanian prime minister, Armand Călinescu, was assassinated.

As would be expected at such a time, matters moved very quickly. Soon after having returned to England, Gubbins was sent to Paris to head up the British Military Mission to the Czech and Polish military forces, which at that time were under the command of French officers. But just six months later he was recalled from France to raise what were known as Independent Companies, which would go on to become British Commandos.

Initially there were ten Independent Companies, raised from volunteers from home-based Territorial Army divisions in April 1940. The intention was to use them for guerrilla-style operations as part of the Allied Campaign in Norway. The companies were short-lived, as they were disbanded after returning to Britain at the end of the campaign.

Gubbins commanded some of these companies in Norway, where he proved to be both a bold and resourceful hands-on leader of his men. He certainly was not afraid to make difficult decisions, even down to dismissing a Guards battalion commander who was not up to the task at hand in the heat of battle. As a result of his actions during the Norwegian campaign, Gubbins was awarded the Distinguished Service Order (DSO).

On his return from Norway, Gubbins had a bit of a reality check, because despite a recommendation for a command position by the commander of all British and Allied troops who had been involved in the Norway campaign, Lieutenant General Claude Auchinleck, he found himself based in the UK, in charge of home forces. But it was still an interesting posting because it involved him forming secret Auxiliary Units, which in essence were a commando force involving both elements of the Home Guard and regular army troops who would be trained and used as sabotage units and, in the case of a German invasion of Britain, would operate behind German lines, causing havoc as best they could.

These Auxiliary Units were the brainchild of Prime Minister Winston Churchill, and answered to general headquarters of the Home Forces command, but from a totally legal point of view, they were part of the Home Guard. The men selected for these secret units were highly trained, and for the work they were expected to carry out – irregular or guerrilla warfare – they certainly needed to be. Gubbins was at somewhat of an advantage in this aspect as he was preparing and training his men for a possible eventuality, rather than a reaction to events that had already taken place, such as Gubbins had experienced at first hand both in Poland and France earlier in the war.

In the event of a German invasion and occupation of mainland Britain, these Auxiliary units would fight in British army uniform, but as a guerrilla force rather than employing basic army tactics. They would be like a private army. They were in fact so secret that Home Guard commanders were not even aware of their existence. Once the Germans had landed on British soil, Auxiliary units would not be part of the initial Home Guard response at defending their local town or village; instead their work would begin once their Home Guard colleagues had been defeated or had surrendered. Then and only then would they begin their work of taking the fight to the enemy by causing maximum disruption against their forces, lines of communication and movements of both troops and equipment. Their actions were intended to be quick, aggressive, violent and decisive, and they were certainly never intended to be used as a long-term resistance movement.

Service in the Auxiliary units could be described as being far from a good choice for a man to make. If they had actually been activated, the work that these men would have been expected to carry out would have been very dangerous. It was estimated that their life expectancy would have been no longer than twelve days after German forces had begun their occupation. If the threat from the enemy was not dangerous enough, they were also under strict instructions not to be captured and taken alive. They had been ordered that if they believed capture by German forces was imminent or seemed likely, they were to kill themselves.

Gubbins' experience and knowledge of guerrilla tactics and warfare was vast and had been gained during the Allied intervention in the Russian Civil War of 1919, and during the Irish War of Independence between 1919 and 1921. He was transferred to the newly formed SOE in November 1940, at the request of Hugh Dalton. His remit was to 'co-ordinate all action by way of sabotage and subversion against the enemy overseas', which was exactly what he had been tasked with doing when in charge of the Auxiliary units. It was now up to him to arrange and organise training facilities; to come up with agreed operating procedures that would be acceptable to both the Admiralty and the Air Ministry. Whilst maintaining these aspects of his role, he also had to establish a close working relationship with members of the Joint Planning Staff.

A humorous anecdote attached to the Auxiliary units saw its men referred to as 'scallywags' and what they did as 'scallywagging'.

It was not all plain sailing for Gubbins as wartime had a habit of ensuring that matters never quite went according to plan, especially when it came to manpower and equipment, which there was never enough of. But there were successes as well. The Shetland Bus operation had been utilised to transport agents working for the SOE into Norway to assist local resistance groups score a notable success with a raid on a heavy water production plant in Norway.

A problem that was not unique to wartime Britain, was the question of what happens when different agencies disagree with each other? How do you get these different agencies to work together, and if you manage to do so, how is it decided who is charge? A good example of this working at its best would be an invasion such as the D-Day Normandy landings, where all three branches of the military – army, air force and the navy – needed to work together, to provide a united front.

In September 1943, a problem arose between three of the country's major departments. The Joint Intelligence Committee, formed on 7 July 1936, was a sub-committee of the Committee of Imperial Defence. During the Second World War, it was the UK's senior intelligence assessment body.

During the Second World War, the General Headquarters Middle East supervised military operations in and around the Mediterranean and the Middle East. It was established in Cairo, just before the outbreak of war, in June 1939, because of the rising tensions throughout Europe. The purpose of the unit was to provide a centralised command structure in a wartime scenario for the three separate army commands that had traditionally been stationed throughout the Middle East and the Mediterranean region. In the event that war did break out, their area of authority was to be increased. The man initially placed in charge was Lieutenant General Sir Archibald Wavell.

The General Headquarters Middle East command came under the control of the Committee of Imperial Defence, who took the decision that all three branches of Britain's armed forces should be collectively responsible for the defence of the Middle East Region. This meant that Admiral Sir Andrew Cunningham from the Royal Navy and Air Chief Marshal Arthur Longmore, had to work alongside Sir Archibald Wavell.

Understanding the importance, but also the potential complexities of such a body, Wavell suggested that a committee, chaired by a government cabinet minister, should be established in the Middle East, to perform the duties delegated to it by the Home Office. This way there would not be a constant need to make contact with the War Cabinet for instructions. Despite Wavell's suggestion being a sensible one, it was not implemented. Instead it was decided to establish a ministerial committee, based in London, with the job of reviewing the changing situation in the Middle East. To assist this process, Oliver Littleton, was appointed as the minister of state for the Middle East on 28 June 1941. His new role was to provide Wavell, Cunningham and Longmore political guidance on such matters as propaganda, subversive warfare, financial budgets and economic warfare.

The last of the three departments was the Foreign Office, which had overall responsibility for foreign affairs.

In September 1943, it was these three bodies that sought to remove the SOE's autonomy in its decision-making ability, especially in the area of operations. The decision was taken to place all SOE field operations under the direction of theatre commanders; this was despite the unequivocal support and backing of Lord Selborne, who between 1942 and 1945, was the minister of economic warfare, which in essence meant that he was in overall charge of the SOE.

For such a clandestine organisation, this was like having one hand tied behind its back. Paramount for them was security, because the fewer people who knew about their very existence or what they did, the safer their agents would be and the more success they were likely to achieve – and more importantly, the less chance there was of somebody betraying their agents.

Sir Charles Hambro, who at the time was the executive head of the SOE, resigned in protest. It was Colin Gubbins who replaced him. Just four months later these same bodies once again tried to dismantle the SOE after it was revealed that their operations had been infiltrated in Holland by elements of German intelligence.

CHAPTER FOUR

The Commencement of the Shetland Bus

On 29 April 1940, with Norway under Nazi occupation, the Norwegian monarch King Haakon VII left Molde aboard HMS *Glasgow,* a light cruiser first commissioned in 1937, and headed for the UK. With him were members of the Norwegian government and the nation's gold reserves (which had been stored in the Norwegian National Bank in Molde). Meanwhile, the fighting against the Germans in the north of Norway continued until the end of May. At about the same time as HMS *Glasgow* left Norway, the first of the Norwegian fishing vessels arrived in Shetland, many of them repeatedly returning to Norway to pick up more refugees. The captains and their crews were more concerned with securing freedom for their fellow Norwegians than they were in their own safety in repeatedly crossing the perilous waters of the North Sea.

The defeat of the British Expeditionary Force in the Battle of France, and the subsequent evacuation of its survivors at Dunkirk in May 1940, greatly angered Churchill. In effort to raise morale and show Nazi Germany that Britain was still a force to be reckoned with, Churchill ordered the Joint Chiefs of Staff to come up with proposals for an offensive against German-occupied Europe. He wanted the men who would carry out these attacks to be specially trained, and to be able to breed fear into the hearts of the enemy by carrying out a reign of terror against nominated targets along the coastline of German-occupied Europe.

Somewhat fortuitously in the circumstances, the highly respected British army officer, Lieutenant Colonel Dudley Clarke, had already submitted a very similar proposal to his boss, the Chief of the Imperial General Staff, General Sir John Dill, who with Churchill's order ringing loudly in his ear, promptly approved Clarke's proposal.

It was decided that this new force of commandos would come under the control of the Combined Operations Headquarters, which was part of the British War Office, and its first commander was Admiral Sir Roger Keyes, who had served in the Royal Navy between 1885 and 1935 and was a veteran of both the Boxer Rising of 1899–1901, and the First World War, during which time he was in command of the Dover Patrol for the final eleven months of the war. He was brought back into service with the Royal Navy in 1940, albeit for only a year, and by which time he was already 68 years old. So it was that in the summer of 1940 a call went out amongst serving members of the British army, who were at the time stationed in Britain and who were looking for excitement and a chance to take the war directly to the enemy. Once volunteers had been selected and had successfully undergone the required level of training to qualify as a commando, then preparations for raids on the coastline of German-occupied Europe could begin in earnest.

In late 1940, the two agencies (SOE and SIS) set up a base in Lerwick, before the SIS moved on to Peterhead. The number of boats arriving in Shetland from Norway had been noticed by the security services, who had realised if there was a route from Norway to Shetland, then there was no reason why it could not operate in the opposite direction. All that was needed was for the captains of the fishing vessels who had brought refugees out of Norway to agree to take their agents back in. Most of them had no problem with this as they intended to return to pick up more refugees in any case, so having a few passengers for company on the long journey was not a problem. This arrangement, although ad hoc, continued throughout the winter months of 1940/1941. But such a way of operating was not conducive to a long-term solution. This was highlighted by the fact that nobody knew how long the war, or the occupation of Norway, was going to continue. So in early 1941, the Shetland Bus became an official entity.

The men put in charge of the group were Major Leslie Mitchell of the British army and Lieutenant David Howarth of the Royal Naval Volunteer Reserve. Their initial choice for a location of their executive headquarters was Flemington House at Weisdale, and a location at Lunna Ness, from where their boats could operate in comparative secrecy, as it possessed a small, sheltered harbour and an even smaller population who were more than happy to 'mind their own business', and not ask too many questions. Lunna House was initially used as accommodation for the boat crews and was a seventeenth-century Laird's house, built for Robert Hunter, a Commissioner of Supply, which in essence meant that he was the local tax collector, in around 1663. It was built on the site of a medieval hall, which in turn had been built on the site of a Viking longhouse.

Major Mitchell remained at Flemington House, whilst Lieutenant Howarth turned Lunna House into the group's operational headquarters. Excluding Mitchell and Howarth, the group's staff consisted of just seven. These included British army sergeants, Almond, Sherwood and Olsen; a stenographer in Norman Edwards, and Harald Albertson, a Norwegian, as the cook, all based at Lunna House, whilst Major Mitchell had two maids for company at Flemington.

Because repair facilities at Lunna were lacking, the operational base was moved to Scalloway in 1942. Major Mitchell left the base in Scalloway in December 1942 and was replaced as leader of operations by Captain Arthur William Sclater. His Norwegian-born wife, Alice, became the welfare officer for the crews who manned the vessels of the Shetland Bus. Although born in Sussex, Sclater's mother was Norwegian, and he had spent many of his boyhood summers holidaying in Norway.

At the outbreak of the war, Sclater had tried to enlist in the Royal Marines, but because his job as a wood pulp agent was considered to be a reserved occupation and vital to the war effort, his request to join up was turned down. It would be nearly two years before his wish was granted, and in 1941 he was called up, given a commission and immediately transferred to the SOE in Shetland.

It was because of his intimate knowledge of Norway and his ability to speak the language that he found himself so assigned. His wife went with him, having also been recruited by the British authorities, but as they still had many relatives in Norway, they arrived in Shetland using the name Captain and Mrs Rogers, so if discovered, the Nazis could not connect them to their family in Norway.

To begin with, the Shetland Bus operation consisted of fourteen Norwegian fishing boats of differing sizes. But the vessel which undertook the first Shetland Bus journey was the *Aksel*, whose captain was August Nærøy. His crew on that inaugural journey which left for Bergen from Hamnavoe, on the west side of Lunna Ness, on 30 August 1941, were Mindor Berge, Ivar Brekke, Andreas Gjertsen, and Bård Grotle.

Flemington House, which was where 'Captain' and Mrs Rogers lived, was ostensibly used for the training of the group's saboteurs, and was where agents waiting to be sent to Norway stayed, and where they were debriefed on their return. Initially it was also used to accommodate incoming refugees, but this practice was stopped as it was recognised that the group's long term security, and the lives of its agents, could potentially be at risk by allowing civilians to be housed with them.

The group's main purpose was to get agents who worked for the SOE into Norway so that they could make contact with the country's resistance groups and supply them with radios, weapons, ammunition, explosives, money and other useful supplies. Once they had completed their mission, they would then be picked up by the Shetland Bus and returned to Shetland to be debriefed. Norwegians who feared they were about to be arrested by the Germans would also be brought out. Special Operations Executive agents also took part in some of the raids carried out by Norwegian resistance groups.

Throughout the course of the war there were a total of twelve raids carried out by British commandos and elements of the SOE along the coast of Norway, which collectively proved to be extremely effective. These raids helped increase the total number of German troops stationed in Norway to some 370,000 men, because of the belief that Britain might try to carry out a full-scale invasion of Norway.

Collectively, the group of men who were the Shetland Bus originally had the name of the Norwegian Naval Independent Unit, but in October 1943, when it officially became part of the Royal Norwegian Navy, it was renamed the Royal Norwegian Naval Special Unit.

One of Norway's resistance fighters was a man named Harald Torsvig. He was responsible for assisting large numbers of Norwegians to escape from Norway and make their way by boat across the North Sea to Shetland. Sometime in early 1941, the British authorities discovered that the German authorities were getting closer to establishing what Torsvig was up to. The SOE sent a fishing boat named *Mars* from Shetland across the North Sea to pick him up and bring him back to Shetland, but despite knowing the danger that he was likely to be in by staying, he refused to go. It was a decision that would ultimately cost him his life, as sometime in April 1941, Torsvig and a number of others who worked with him, were arrested. They were all subsequently put on trial before a German military court in Oslo. A number of them, including Torsvig, were found guilty and executed by firing squad on 26 November 1941. Sadly, it is not known where their bodies were buried, and the German authorities, past or present, have never revealed their final resting places.

Word of the events in Norway had reached the German High Command in Berlin, and they were not happy. It was decided that the efforts to prevent the seaborne escape of Norwegians to Shetland had to be increased. To this end, more German soldiers were deployed to Norwegian coastal regions, with the hope that this would be a sufficient deterrent in greatly reducing, if not totally preventing, the exodus of Norwegians to Shetland.

One of the main locations in Norway where the boats of the Shetland Bus operation arrived at, and departed from, was Alesund, in the Møre og Romsdal county. Somehow the German authorities got to hear of the movements to and from Alesund, or 'Little London', as the Germans liked to refer to it. In an attempt to deal effectively with this situation, members of the Gestapo were sent to Alesund to try to identify those involved in the movements between Norway and the Shetlands. The main way the German authorities gleaned their information was through the use of paid informants; sadly this was usually Norwegians.

All the crews of the Shetland Bus boats were Norwegian. This was mainly because they knew the routes they had to take, but also because if these boats were stopped by German naval vessels, it would be natural that the men on board them would be Norwegian.

One of the most prominent men involved in the Shetland Bus operations was Leif Larsen, a well-known individual, respected and liked by many who met and knew him, and a man who loved his country. He was quite possibly one of the most highly decorated, and famous Shetland Bus operatives. Before his heroics in the North Sea, he had volunteered to serve with Finnish forces in the Winter War with Russia, which took place between 30 November 1939 and 13 March 1940.

During the German invasion of Norway in April 1940, he was a soldier in the Norwegian army and stationed at Kongsvinger

Fortress. Sometime after arriving in the UK he was officially made a sub-lieutenant in the Norwegian navy.

He escaped from German-occupied Norway on board the fishing boat MOTIG 1, arriving in Shetland on 11 February 1941. There he joined the Norwegian Naval Independent Unit, the official name for what became more commonly known as the Shetland Bus, and underwent training in different locations in both England and Scotland.

He was part of Kompani Linge, and after completing his training he returned to Lerwick on board the *St Magnuson* on 19 August 1941 and less than a month later, on 14 September 1941, he undertook his first Shetland Bus operation as part of the crew of the *Siglaos,* which was captained by Petter Salen. Just two months after that, on 8 November 1941, he experienced his first trip as a captain when he sailed the M/K *Arthur* from Shetland with his handpicked crew. This included Palmer Bjornoy, Leif Kinn, Arne Kinn, Kare Iversen, Karsten Sangolt, Nils Nipen, and Otto Pletten. Other than the usual inclement weather of the North Sea, there was nothing unusual about the outward journey from Shetland, nor when they arrived in Norway. It was during the return journey to Shetland that disaster struck. In the difficult weather of the North Sea they ran into a storm, and crew member Karsten Sangolt was blown overboard and lost to the sea. This was exactly the type of danger that every crew faced each time they went to sea as part of the Shetland Bus operation.

Larsen had a somewhat charmed life during his wartime exploits. On 20 October 1941, he was second in command on the minelayer, *Nordsjoen,* when it sank in inclement weather off the coast of west Norway. Thankfully, every member of the crew survived. They were picked up by the M/K *Arthur* and taken into Shetland, where they arrived on 31 October 1941. The irony here was that Larsen would subsequently go on to skipper the *Arthur,* which he would sail on numerous other occasions before having to scuttle her in the Trondheim Fjord in October 1942, after the failed attempt at attacking the German battleship, *Tirpitz.*

On 23 March 1943, Larsen was the skipper of the M/K *Bergholm*, which had been on a mission to Traena in Norway. They had begun their return journey to Shetland when they were attacked by German aircraft. The *Bergholm* was lost in the attack and several of her crew were wounded, but despite their injuries all of them took to the boats. When they were attacked they were nearer to Norway than they were Shetland, so they naturally headed towards the Norwegian coastline. After several days of rowing and living off very basic rations, they came ashore near Alesund, but not long after their arrival, one of the crew, Nils Vika, died of the wound sustained in the attack on the *Bergholm*. Besides Larsen and Vika, the other crew members were: Andreas Faeroy, Johannes Kalvo, Finn Clausen, Gunnar Clausen, Odd Hansen, and William Enoksen.

Larsen managed to get a message back to Shetland about the fate of the *Bergholm*, and, after hiding out with sympathetic local families for some two weeks, he and his crew were rescued by a Royal Navy motor torpedo boat and safely returned to Lerwick in Shetland. Each of those who had looked after Larsen and his crew had done so at great risk to themselves and their families. If the German authorities had discovered what the local people had done, entire families would have no doubt been executed for their loyalty.

In the latter months of 1943, Larsen was put in charge of one of the three fast-moving submarine chasers that had been supplied by the USA. The chasers were transported by liberty ships across the Atlantic Ocean, arriving in Belfast in early October 1943, where they were placed back in the water. On 14 October, the three ships sailed in convoy up the Firth of Clyde, before arriving at the US naval base at Rosneath still with their American crews. It was only on their arrival that they were informed that their job was to train Larsen and his colleagues how to use and operate the chasers and their equipment. After completing a week's training, the American sailors handed over command to the Norwegians. Their work was done.

Larsen and his men sailed their newly acquired chasers to Scalloway in Shetland, where they were refitted for their new role. The depth charge racks, anti-submarine rocket launchers, 20mm cannon, and the depth charge projectors were all removed. A 2-pounder gun, along with two .50 calibre machine guns were added to the vessels, and they were renamed, *Hessa, Hitra* and the *Vigra,* after three islands off the west coast of Norway. The latter of the three vessels was commanded by Larsen, the others by Petter Salen and Ingvald Eidsheim.

These were no ordinary vessels; not only did they have an impressive top speed, which saw them cut through the waves of the North Sea, but they required a crew of twenty-six to run them. They replaced the previously used fleet of civilian fishing boats which until that point had run the operation of the Shetland Bus. An interesting point about the chasers was that despite completing more than 100 missions to German-occupied Norway, the only action any of the three vessels saw was when the *Hessa* was inadvertently attacked by a Canadian aircraft, whose pilot mistook her as a German E-boat.

By the time the war had ended, Larsen had made fifty-two trips to Norway in the *Vigra*, many of which were undertaken in atrocious weather conditions, safely delivering and collecting agents, refugees and equipment on every occasion.

United States Admiral Harold Rainsford Stark, Chief of Naval Operations between 1 August 1939 and 26 March 1942 and Commander of the United States Naval Forces Europe (with his headquarters being in London) from April 1942, was placed in charge of the United States Twelfth Fleet in October 1943 and supervised the US navy's participation in the Normandy landings in June 1944. Later in the war, an officer from his headquarters writing about the three chasers, noted the following about them:

It would be difficult to sum up the value of these three craft in their contribution to the Allies. Hundreds of tons of stores and supplies have been delivered to Resistance groups. An enemy plane has been shot down. Countless agents have been taken in and out and great numbers of marooned allied airmen, including Americans, have been helped to evade the Gestapo. Despite very heavy weather the ships have required minimum repairs.

By the end of the war, Larsen had become the most highly decorated Allied naval officer of the Second World War, with his eleven wartime awards. British awards included the DSO, the DSC, the Distinguished Service Medal (DSM) and Bar. From a grateful Norwegian nation he was awarded the Norwegian War Cross with Two Swords (a gallantry decoration awarded for extraordinary brave actions or extraordinary leadership during combat), St Olav's Medal with Oak Branch and the War Medal with Three Stars, and the Defence Medal 1940–1945. From the US he received the Medal of Freedom, and was also awarded medals by Finland. He held the naval rank of lieutenant commander.

At the time, no other man, British or foreign, had ever received all these British military honours. It is conceivable that had he been British he may well have been awarded the Victoria Cross for his wartime exploits, but as a Norwegian he was not entitled to it.

Lieutenant David Howarth, second in command of the British naval base in Shetland, described Larsen as 'One of the most remarkable personalities of the entire Second World War'.

After the war, Howarth (who at the outbreak of the Second World War had been a war correspondent for the BBC) wrote a number of books, one of them being *The Shetland Bus – A Second World War Epic of Escape, Survival and Adventure* (1951), about his involvement with the Shetland Bus and the men who were part of it and who worked alongside him.

With the war finally at end and German forces having surrendered, 9 May 1945 saw two of the submarine chasers donated to the Shetland Bus by the USA, and the *Hitra* and *Eidsheim* entered the harbour of Lyngoy, near Bergen, in what was by then a liberated and free Norway.

During the years of its existence, the Shetland Bus made a total of 198 journeys to Norway, delivering 192 agents and hundreds of tons of weapons and other supplies. More often than not these were return journeys, the boats rarely returned to Shetland empty handed. A total of 373 refugees, who either wanted to escape from Norway, or from the occupying German forces, were brought out, along with 73 agents. But all of this hard and dangerous work came at a price: the deaths of 44 members of the Shetland Bus.

If any of those men still had a voice they would all have said that their death had been a price worth paying for what had been collectively achieved by the Shetland Bus, and what it had meant to so many people.

The men who manned these boats were extremely brave individuals, facing the possibility of death every time they put to sea. Not just because of the weather conditions they had to endure, but the darkness, the possibility of being discovered by enemy aircrafts or vessels, and the not knowing who was waiting for them on their arrival in Norway. They must have had nerves of steel to be able to survive making such journeys time and time again.

CHAPTER FIVE

Norwegian Agents

The following is a list of Norwegians who worked as agents for the British-run Special Operations Executive during the Second World War. Most if not all of them would have at some stage been involved with the Shetland Bus, either as a crew member on one of the many boats used in the operation, or as an agent who was dropped off or picked up by a Shetland Bus boat.

I do not suggest for one second that this is a comprehensive list of Norwegians who served as such agents, but it is certainly a very large percentage of them. If you discover a name who you think or know should have been included in this list, then you have my apologies, as the omission of any such individual is nothing more than an oversight on my behalf.

Where I have already written about an individual elsewhere in this book, I have not included him within this chapter.

Alf Aakre was born in Norway in 1917. He took part in Operation Carhampton and survived the war.

Johannes Sigfred Andersen was both a member of the Norwegian resistance and of the Kompani Linge. He had managed to acquire the unusual nickname of 'Gulosten', which when translated into English, said 'Yellow Cheese'. The nickname had been acquired as a child. When he was only 10 years old he was made a Ward of

Court and sent to the Toftes Gave School, which was situated on the island of Helgoya in the middle of Lake Mjosa. Whilst there he received food parcels from home, a necessity for all the boys, as food, even at the school, was at a premium. The main content of Andersen's parcels was yellow cheese, hence how he acquired his nickname.

The Toftes Gave School was strict, yet the next educational establishment he was sent to took things to a whole new level. Andersen was 14 years old when he began attending the Bastoy School for maladjusted boys. Discipline and conditions were so bad at the school that in 1915 some twenty-nine boys rebelled against their abusive treatment and went on the rampage. The situation was so bad that staff at the school were unable to deal with the incident and a combination of police officers and soldiers from the Norwegian army were called in to quell the rioting.

A year after starting at the school, when he was still only 15, his mother died, but for some unknown reason he was not informed of her death until more than a week after she had been buried. He was not impressed at all. When the enormity of what he had been told finally sank in, he went ballistic and smashed up the warden's office, leading to him needing to be physically restrained by a number of members of staff. His punishment was a period of isolation in a dark cell, something which he experienced on more than one occasion whilst a pupil at the school.

He married when he was just 18 years old, but it was a short-lived affair. His young wife, Lovise Kristine Klausen, eventually left him when he found himself out of work and money was hard to come by, and she wanted a more secure financial future.

His life of criminality began in earnest in 1921, when he got together with some old school friends from Toftes Gave, and they began to smuggle alcohol and spirits into Norway in fishing vessels. It all came to an end for him when the Norwegian police discovered what he was doing and he became a wanted man. He had to make good his escape to Germany. Once there, he carried on his involvement in smuggling, but this time he was involved in the delivery of the spirits and not its distribution. The Norwegian authorities became aware that Andersen was in Germany so they applied to extradite him and police sailed to Hamburg to pick him up and return him to Norway. As the boat he was on entered the Oslofjord, he jumped overboard and managed to escape.

Throughout the 1920s and 1930s he continued with his life of criminality, which involved burglaries and safe-cracking. Between 1919 and 1937, he served nine prison sentences, spending a total of seven years in custody. All he had to show for the life he had led was to be a household name throughout Norway, but for all the wrong reasons. Andersen remarried in 1939 and had another son, and on the day Germany invaded Norway, was released from prison.

It would be fair to say that Andersen, or Ostein, another surname that he was known by, was quite a controversial character. Before the war he was a well-known criminal and had been for many years. One of his attributes, which appears to have appealed to the SOE, was his skill as an assassin.

The German invasion of Norway saw him drawn into the war intentionally or otherwise. He had a furniture workshop that was used by the Norwegian resistance movement to store their weapons, and he helped them when they went on raids to loot German military stores.

In 1942, Andersen shot dead a man by the name of Raymond Colberg, who was a well-known informant for the German Abwehr, and then escaped to Sweden. In March 1941, Colberg had discovered an illegal radio transmitter in the Sandefjord area. After informing his Abwehr bosses, eight local resistance members were arrested, three of whom, Oivind Ask, Andreas Bertnes and Johan Midttun, were shot by firing squad on 4 December 1941.

After escaping to Sweden, Andersen made his way to the UK where he became a member of the SOE. He later went on to work for the Royal Norwegian Navy on one of their motor torpedo boats that were involved in attacking German shipping off the Norwegian coast.

Despite his criminal record, he and King Haakon VII of Norway were good friends, to such an extent, that the king helped Andersen's carpentry business financially.

Andreas Aubert was both a member of the Norwegian resistance movement and, from 1942, a member of the Kompani Linge. His older brother Kristian had also been an active member of the Norwegian resistance movement, but had been captured by the Gestapo in 1942 and tortured to death at the Grini detention camp in Baerum, which the Germans used as a concentration camp during their occupation.

Andreas Aubert was a member of the Oslo Gang, which was a sabotage group under the command of Gunnar Sønsteby. For his wartime service he was awarded the War Cross with Sword, the St Olav's Medal with Oak Branch, and His Majesty the King's Commemorative Medal with Bar 1940–1945.

Torfinn Bjørnaas was studying engineering sciences at the Technische Hochschule in Aachen, Germany, until April 1940, when he returned to his native Norway on holiday, and whilst he was there, he found himself on the receiving end of the German invasion.

He had completed his compulsory military service in His Majesty The King's Guard in 1936, so joined his fellow countrymen in trying to defend his country against the Nazi invasion. Once Norwegian forces had surrendered, Bjørnaas did not hang around to be captured and spend the rest of the war in a prisoner of war camp, and instead set off for Sweden. After initially having failed in his attempt at reaching Sweden, he and a few others decided they would make their way to England, which they did, but by taking the slightly unusual route of travelling via India.

He enlisted in the Kompani Linge and underwent his training in both England and Scotland, before being sent back to Norway via the Shetland Bus to conduct acts of sabotage against German occupying forces. His time back in Norway saw him take part in sabotage missions at Sulitjelma and Terningmoen, and more famously, for the Thamshavn Line train sabotage in 1943. This involved four separate acts on the railway lines in Orkdal, which were carried out by Bjørnaas and his colleagues from Kompani Linge in an attempt to prevent the Germans from obtaining the pyrites which were being mined at Lokken Vert, a village in the municipality of Orkland in Trondelag county.

The Lokken mine was well established and by the time of the Second World War it had been in production for nearly 300 years. It was also directly connected by railway line to the port at Thamshavn, and before the war, Germany had been one of the mine's biggest customers. With the war then in full swing, Germany was no longer a customer that Norway wanted to trade with. But after occupying the country, German forces quickly secured control of the mine. The race was now on to prevent them from taking anything out of the mine and transporting it back to Germany to assist in their war effort.

The first target for the group was the transformer station for the electric railway at Bardshaug. If the transformer station was put out of use, no trains could use the track. The team for this part of the operation was Torleif Grong, Per Getz and Peter Deinboll. They had arrived in Norway at Bjornor on Fosen, having made their way across the North Sea on one of the boats of the Shetland Bus. From Bjornor, they walked towards their final destination at Namdalseid, being passed en route by German army trucks, one of which offered them a lift. Deciding that it might be a safe and sure way of getting to Namdalseid, they accepted, despite the fact that each of their rucksacks contained large amounts of explosives which they had brought with them from Shetland.

The three men eventually arrived at Orkdal on the evening of 4 May 1942, placed their timed explosives in the transformer station and left. They were timed to detonate at 5 am the following day, which they did, by which time, the three-man team was well on its way to Sweden, via Trondheim and Meraker.

The second part of the operation was the port at Thamshavn. The team on this occasion was Peter Deinboll, Bjorn Pedersen and Olav Saettem. Initially the three men stayed at the home of Deinboll's parents, before moving on to a log cabin high up in the forest which surrounded Thamshavn. There they were relatively safe, or as safe as they could be in the circumstances. They had the assistance of members of the local resistance movement who brought them much-needed supplies. It was obvious to them early on that their target at the harbour was much too heavily guarded to blow it up, so instead they decided to blow up one of the ships in the harbour, which just happened to be the D/S *Nordfahrt*, a cargo ship that would be full of pyrites waiting to be transported to Germany.

On the evening of 24 February 1943, the three men sailed out to the *Nordfahrt* in a small rowing boat and placed limpet mines on to its hull, which were timed to detonate at 4 pm the following day. The next morning, another cargo vessel arrived in the harbour which then meant that the *Nordfahrt* had to be moved out of the harbour and into the fjord. When the explosives detonated, it caused damage to the ship but did not sink it, and a tug boat was able to get a line on her, and tow her into land.

Neither of the first two attacks were what might have been termed as major successes. The Germans would not have been too inconvenienced for long by either attack. The fact that none of the men had been captured was a success in itself.

The target for what was to be the third and final part of the raid was the Lokken mine itself. This required a total of seven men, once again led by Peter Deinboll. If it did not go according to plan, as in the initial explosion causing sufficient damage, the seven men were to blow up the locomotives that were used to pull railway carriages out of the mine, which would greatly affect the supply of pyrites available to the German authorities.

The seven men were parachuted in on the sometime in early October, landing at Svorkdalskjolen, and not for the first time hid out in long cabins in the forest as they prepared and planned the finite details of their raid. Unfortunately they were discovered by German forces but managed to escape, and that was the end of the plans for the attack on the Lokken mines.

These men were determined individuals and certainly not the type to shy away from a fight. On 31 October 1943, they had made plans to blow up a number of train locomotives at different locations, one of which was Lokken. Once again things did not quite go according to plan, and although four locomotives were blown up, others were not, simply because they were not in the locations that the men expected them to be. In another attempt at blowing up a locomotive, things did not go right yet again. This time sufficient explosives had not been attached to the locomotive, which resulted in the damage caused being nowhere near as extensive as had been expected. One of the team, Odd Nilsen, was killed in the attempt, and the rest of the team split up and left the area, but one member, Paal Skjaerpe, was discovered by the Germans in Hovin and handed over to the Gestapo in Trondheim, where he was tortured. He did not talk, and miraculously survived the war.

In the early part of 1944, a three-man team returned to Norway, entering the country from Sweden, to destroy the last of the locomotives which were being used at the Lokken mine. The last two trains were blown up by the three-man sabotage group on 9 and 31 May 1944, but the Germans managed to bring in other locomotives from both France and Germany to replace them. However, their ability to remove large quantities of pyrites from the mine and ship them to Germany was effectively brought to an end because of the time it took to bring the new locomotives to Norway, and the issues which arose over the differing size of the rail gauge meant that the war was over before the matter was fully resolved.

There was a sad aftermath to all of this, which had originated out of the decision to send in saboteurs to halt the large quantities of pyrites being extracted from the Lokken mine and shipped back to Germany, rather than let the RAF send in their bomber aircraft to do it. The Norwegian resistance movement had won the argument to do it by the use of saboteurs, because of their desire not to see Norwegian civilians killed in the bombings.

Peter Blessing Deinboll, Peter Vogelius Deinbolls' father, was the chief engineer at the Lokken mine, and after the attack in 1942 on the railway transformer, it was he who was tasked with repairing it and getting it up and running again. But instead he took his family, fled to Sweden, and worked for the Norwegian resistance movement.

After the war ended and Norway had been liberated from her Nazi occupation, Peter Blessing Deinboll and his family returned home, but not to the reception they might have been expecting. He was blamed for the wartime destruction caused at the mine and was refused his old job back. His home had been given to another family, and other properties he owned had been auctioned off. It would be fifty-eight years before the owners of the mine, the Orkla Group, issued an apology to the Deinboll family for their treatment of Peter Blessing Deinboll and his family, by which time both senior and junior Deinboll were long since dead.

For his wartime endeavours, Peter Vogelius Deinboll was awarded the Norwegian honours of the War Cross with Sword, and the St Olav's Medal with Oak Branch, along with the British awards of the DSO and Bar and the MC. He died on 8 November 1944, when a flight he was a passenger on from the UK to Norway disappeared.

Theodor Borchgrevink was still only 16 years old at the beginning of the Second World War. He was born in the suburb of Brooklyn, New York, but was brought up in Stabekk, west of Oslo.

Enrolled as a student at the Norwegian Institute of Technology, his studies came to an end in 1941, when the Institute was closed and he decided to leave Norway for England, after having first escaped to neighbouring Sweden. He initially enlisted in the Royal Norwegian Air Force in exile, but in the final stages of the war he became a member of the Kompani Linge.

Einar Boyesen was a member of the Norwegian resistance movement during the Second World War.

Eilert Eilertsen was known to be a member of the Norwegian resistance movement, who had to flee to the UK when the Germans discovered his activities. It is believed he escaped with the help of the Shetland Bus, however, little recorded information is available in relation to his wartime achievements.

Erik Gjems-Onstad joined the Norwegian resistance movement at the beginning of the German occupation of Norway, and escaped to Sweden, but was arrested there for his resistance involvement and activity in 1941 and sent to the UK. Once there he joined Kompani Linge and after successfully completing his training in 1943, was sent back to Norway on board a vessel of the Shetland Bus, as part of 'Lark', the code word that was given to the group of men who were sent to Trondheim as part of the preparations for a future possible Allied invasion. His specific role was to establish radio contact between the Lark group and London. He remained with the Lark group in Trondelag until the end of the war.

His other activities whilst in Norway included weapons smuggling and putting plans in place for the sinking of the German battleship, *Tirpitz,* which was in the comparative safety of Norwegian waters. He was also involved in plotting the murder of the Norwegian collaborator, Ivar Grande, who was a Norwegian police officer and an agent for the Gestapo in Trondheim. He was responsible for infiltrating numerous resistance groups, which in turn led to the execution of many of his fellow Norwegians, who were members of these groups.

It is not known for certain who was responsible for assassinating Grande, but he was shot dead in Alesund on 11 December 1944 and SOE agents or Milorg members were strongly suspected of involvement. Erik Gjems-Onstad had become increasingly frustrated by the activities of collaborators such as Grande, and had been vocal in advocating their assassination.

Erling Halle became a member of the Norwegian resistance movement after German forces invaded Norway in April 1940, and later enlisted in the Kompani Linge. After completing his training, he returned to Norway on board a vessel of the Shetland Bus. He was subsequently arrested by the Gestapo on 14 November 1944, initially being held at Mollergata 19 until 30 December that year, and after that at the Grini detention camp until Norway was liberated on 8 May 1945. One of his wartime awards was the St Olav's Medal with Oak Branch.

Nils Uhlin Hansen was a noted athlete before the war, and competed in the long jump at both national and international level. He would have undoubtedly competed at the 1940 Summer Olympic Games in Tokyo, Japan, had they not been cancelled due to the outbreak of the Second World War.

During the Second World War he became a member of the Norwegian resistance movement in 1940, but with the Gestapo hot on his heels he had to escape from Norway, which he did, initially to Sweden in 1941, before eventually making it to England in 1942, where he became part of the Kompani Linge. He returned to Norway on one of the boats of the Shetland Bus to carry out sabotage missions throughout Norway, of which there were many during the second half of 1944 and early 1945.

One of the main targets of these sabotage missions was to knock out trains and railway lines, especially in the north of the country, as Germany began the large operation of retreating her troops.

Hansen was shot dead by German forces on 10 January 1945, when he was discovered in a log cabin at Forsetvollan in Budal. This incident had begun when the same German troops had stopped and spoken to a skier in Singsas. After questioning him, they let him go, but then followed the tracks he had left in the snow, which led straight to the cabin where Hansen was hiding.

Two days after his death, colleagues of Hansen from the Kompani Linge unit were responsible for what has become known as the Jorstadelva Bridge sabotage. They blew up the bridge to cause disruption to the Nordland railway line in Snasa, to ensure that German forces in Norway could not be moved in large numbers to reinforce the final defence of Germany. They achieved their aim when, six hours after the bridge had been destroyed, a train carrying a number of German soldiers crashed into the river below the bridge as the driver of train had failed to notice in time that the bridge had been blown. Approximately seventy-eight German soldiers and two Norwegian civilians were killed in the crash. Another 100 German soldiers were injured. It remains to this day the deadliest rail crash incident in Norway. Although most of those involved in sabotaging the bridge were Norwegians, the man in charge of the operation was an American, Major William Colby, of the Office of Strategic Services, the American equivalent of Britain's SOE.

After the war, Colby was invited to join the newly formed Central intelligence Agency, which he happily accepted. He went on to become the Deputy Director of the Central Intelligence for Operation in 1973 for six months before becoming the Director of Central Intelligence on 4 September 1973, a position he held until 30 January 1976, serving under presidents Richard Nixon and Gerald Ford.

Knut Magne Haugland was a member of the Norwegian resistance movement. Before the war he had already enlisted in the Norwegian army, and once Germany invaded Norway he was in the thick of the fighting, taking part in battles around the Narvik area during what is known as the Norwegian Campaign.

After Germany had defeated Norway militarily, Haugland found himself a job at the Hovding Radiofabrikk factory near Oslo, which in part was also a cover for the Norwegian resistance movement. He was eventually arrested by the Statspolitiet, an armed police force made up of Norwegians that was established on 1 June 1941, a force which operated independently of the day-to-day Norwegian civilian police force. He was yet another who managed to escape from German custody after being arrested and detained. Initially he made his way to Sweden, before carrying on to England where he, like many others, enlisted in the Kompani Linge.

Haugland's most notable sabotage mission was the famous raid on the Norsk Hydro Rjukan plant at Vemork, which produced heavy water. The code name for the mission was Operation Grouse and involved Haugland and three other men, Arne Kjelstrup, Jens-Anton Poulsson and Claus Helberg, who were parachuted into Norway over Hardangervidda on 18 October 1942. Their instructions were to wait until they were joined by British airborne forces, also being sent over from the UK, who would be joining them in the raid on the Vemork Norsk Hydro chemical plant in Telemark. Their code name was Operation Freshman, and their part of the plan required them to land near to the target as close as they possibly could, by glider, set their explosives and then escape into Sweden.

Knut Haukelid led the team that was responsible for the sinking of the Norwegian vessel, SF *Hydro*, on 20 February 1944, on Lake Tinn. The *Hydro* was a passenger and vehicle ferry, but on this occasion it was believed to be carrying heavy water for use in the German war effort. One of Haukelid's team managed to board the vessel, plant explosives on the inside of the ferry's keel, and get out again. Soon after, and with the ferry in deep water, the explosives detonated and the *Hydro* quickly sank to the bottom of the lake.

Despite the efforts and intentions to keep Norwegian casualties to a minimum, fourteen of them, crew and passengers on board the vessel, were killed, along with four German soldiers.

In 2005, a barrel containing heavy water was recovered from the floor of the lake. It was suggested that the quantities of heavy water on the *Hydro* were too small to be of any value for a weapons programme that the Germans were involved in, but however much heavy water was on board, it was being moved for a reason.

Claus Helberg was one of a large group of Norwegians who escaped from their country on board vessels of the Shetland Bus, and made their way to the UK in January 1942. On his arrival, he was part of a group who volunteered and were judged suitable for commando training. After extensive training in Scotland, he was deemed ready for operational services, and in October 1942, he, along with four other Norwegians, returned to Norway when they were parachuted into the Rjukan region. The team's code name was 'Swallow' and its mission was to guide a British commando unit to a hydroelectric plant at Vemork, where it was believed heavy water was being developed for use in a German atomic bomb programme.

For a number of reasons, the British commandos never arrived, but Helberg and his small team remained in Norway and gathered whatever useful information that they could about German activities in the area. One night, Helberg was discovered by a German soldier, who chased after him. Both men were on skis, with the chase continuing for a number of hours, during which time Helberg skied off a small cliff and broke one of his arms on landing, but having shot and wounded the German soldier, he managed to escape.

He was helped by locals in both Mogen and Rauland, before making a truly remarkable decision which showed the nerves of steel that men such as Helberg possessed. In Rauland he went to the local German headquarters and managed to convince them that he had been out searching for saboteurs when he had fallen and broken his arm. Amazingly, the Germans to whom he told his story believed him and took him to see one of their doctors. After the doctor had carried out his initial inspection, Helberg was then taken by the German soldiers to a hospital at Dalen, and after having his wounds dealt with they took him to a hotel where he was given a room.

Helberg made an extremely dangerous decision to do what he did, because if they had asked a few more questions of him, such as where he lived, did he have any family who could come and pick him up, why was he looking for saboteurs and who asked him to do so, he may have well been found out to be lying.

By sheer misfortune, Josef Terboven, the Nazi Commissioner of occupied Norway, arrived at the same hotel where Helberg had been put up. Terboven, apparently suffering from a severe inferiority complex, ordered a local woman to have dinner with him. Possibly fearing what he had in mind for afters, she refused. Terboven was obviously not happy about being turned down so robustly and publicly, and decided to react somewhat childishly, which at the same time was also potentially dangerous for all those concerned. He ordered that everybody at the hotel should be arrested and sent to the Grini detention camp for questioning and internment if such a punishment were deemed necessary. Through no fault of his own, Helberg now found himself in an extremely precarious position, because he knew that the camp was not going to be an easy place to escape from, and if his true identity as a resistance fighter was discovered, he would be tortured then executed.

He needed to think and act quickly. A bus had been called to ferry everybody from the hotel to the concentration camp. When it was his turn, he got on the bus, calmly took a seat at the back, and a short while into the journey, he jumped out and escaped, re-injuring his broken arm in the process, but at least he was alive.

For his wartime service he was awarded a total of eleven medals from six different countries: Norway, Denmark, France, the USA, the Soviet Union and the UK.

Kasper Idland escaped Norway on a boat of the Shetland Bus which left Egersund in September 1941 and made its way to Shetland. It was not long before he enlisted in Kompani Linge and trained as a commando. Just five months later he found himself back in Norway as part of Operation Anklet.

He was very active during the course of Nazi Germany's occupation of his homeland: he was involved in the raid on the heavy water plant at Vemork, in February 1943 and between 1944 and 1945, he was a member of the Norwegian resistance group, Vestige IV, in and around the Norwegian town of Egersund, in the Rogaland county.

From March 1945 until the German surrender in May 1945, he was active in one of the Varg resistance groups, who received supplies of weapons, ammunition and food dropped by parachute from allied aircraft. Idland survived the war and emigrated to the USA in 1955.

Kare Iversen was born in the municipality of Flatanger in central Norway. His father was a sea pilot, often referred to by other names such as harbour pilot or simply pilot; in essence a sailor who helped manoeuvre large ships through dangerous or congested waters, such as harbours or river mouths. Such men possessed local detailed information, such as depths, currents and hidden underwater obstacles.

As a young boy, Kare often joined his father on his pilot boat, especially during the school holidays, where he would spend many happy hours watching and helping his father do his job.

He was a 21-year-old fisherman when the Germans invaded Norway in April 1940, and like many young Norwegians he was so incensed that a foreign power was now in control of his country that he joined the Norwegian resistance movement. It is not known how, but his affiliation was soon discovered and he found himself on the Germans wanted list. For his family's safety he had to go into hiding.

In August 1941, he 'took' his father's boat, the 42-ft long *Villa II,* and along with three other local men he escaped across the North Sea to the UK, arriving in Shetland. But the journey did not go ahead without its problems. The *Villa II* left Iverden in Flatanger at just after 8 pm, after the German vessel which patrolled the seas in the immediate vicinity, a commandeered Norwegian armed whale catcher, had finished its patrol.

Two days into the journey and everything was fine, even the weather had been favourable to them. It was during the third day that their problems began, when the *Villa II* was spotted by a German flying boat pilot who wasted no time in beginning his attack, which lasted for some twenty minutes as he flew back and forth past the Norwegian vessel. The machine-gun fire from the German flying boat riddled the boat's hull and wheel house. Luckily for the *Villa II*, the seas were quite rough at the time, which prevented the German aircraft from landing. Thankfully for Iversen and his friends, the Germans gave up their attack and their attempts at landing and simply flew off.

After having assessed the damage to the boat and checked that he and the others were all well, Iversen soon had his boat up and running again and on its way to Scotland. He knew that he had to get there as quickly as possible, so he ran the boat's engine at full capacity. It was nearly two days before they spotted land, and even then they were uncertain as to where they were. After making their way ashore, they discovered that they were on Fellar, one of the sparsely populated north Shetland islands.

After being questioned by the authorities in Lerwick as to their identities and intentions, they were sent along with a group of other Norwegians to London, where Iversen joined and undertook training with Kompani Linge.

The next four years would see him undertake numerous crossings of the North Sea, many of which would have been in atrocious conditions. During his time with the Special Operations Executive and Kompani Linge, he undertook a total of fifty-seven trips across the North Sea on a number of different vessels, transporting agents backwards and forwards, along with equipment, supplies and refugees.

Initially he was allocated to the crew of Leif Larsen on the M/B/*Arthur*, with whom he sailed on several occasions. His main role was that of ship's engineer, undoubtedly an important job on any boat. If something went wrong in the North Sea a boat simply could not afford to be immobile for too long, so an experienced and competent engineer was invaluable.

At other times he was also part of the crew of the fishing vessels *Sigalos, Feje, Harald, Heland,* and *Vigraand*, as well as the American-provided submarine chaser, the *Hesse*.

It was also during his time working for the SOE that he met and married Christine Slater from Scalloway, which after the war is where they set up home and lived out the rest of their lives.

Ingolf Johannesen was a member of the crew of KNM *Hitra*, one of the Shetland Bus's new vessels provided by the USA in 1943, which they had used as submarine chasers. For the Shetland Bus operation it meant journeys could be completed more quickly, and potentially in a much safer environment.

Johannesen survived the war and passed away in 1992 at the age of 94.

Alv Marius Johnsen took part in the Battle of Bagan during the invasion of Norway by German forces in April 1940. But after Norway surrendered and Germany occupied the country, he helped set up an illegal newspaper, which was a dangerous enterprise to be involved in, especially if the Germans knew what you were doing. In the latter part of 1941, with the Germans closing in on him, he had to escape from his beloved Norway. His choice of destination was the UK, but rather than take the most direct route via the North Sea in one of the boats of the Shetland Bus, he chose the slightly longer and complicated route of going via Sweden, Russia, India and Canada, and then the UK. Like many of his compatriots who had made their way there, he enlisted in Kompani Linge and ended up serving on a motor torpedo boat as part of the Shetland Bus, between May and December 1944, in one of the three vessels which had been donated to the SOE by the Americans.

In early 1945, he was parachuted into Norway to help train and instruct one of Norway's premier resistance movements, the Milorg, a role he continued with until the end of the war. He survived the war and went on to have a long and distinguished military career in the Norwegian armed forces.

Fredrik Kayser had been in neighbouring Finland during the early stages of the war and just happened to choose 9 April 1940 as his date of return to Norway, the same day Germany invaded his country. As many of his fellow countrymen did, he took up arms and fought against the invading Germans. Just two weeks after returning home, he found himself involved in the Battle of Skjervet in Granvin, which was a small municipality in the Hordaland county of Norway. The battle was won by the Germans and the Norwegian forces soon found themselves having to retreat to the village of Gudvangen in the municipality of Aurland, before those who had survived dispersed to different parts of the country. Kayser made his way to the city of Bergen, where he became involved in the printing and publishing of an illegal newspaper.

Life became more difficult for him in Norway, and he began to believe that it would only be a matter of time before he was discovered and arrested by the Gestapo. To make sure that did not happen, he escaped to the UK, via the Shetland Bus and some friendly and helpful Norwegian sailors in September 1941, where he enlisted in the Kompani Linge. After completing his training in Scotland, he was sent back to Norway in December 1941 as part of Operation Anklet. Kayser and two other Kompani Linge soldiers were parachuted into Norway, where they landed on the Nevlandsheia Plateau in Gjesdal. Their intended target was the Sola Air Station in Western Norway, but the mission never took place.

In 1942 and 1943, he was involved in the failed mission of Operation Freshman and the successful Operation Gunnerside, which involved the heavy water facility at Vemork. For his part in the mission, King George VI awarded Kayser the Military Medal.

Kayser returned to England, where he underwent training in the use of one-manned midget submarines. His intended mission was to attack German shipping that was docked in the harbour of Maloy. But it had to be aborted when unknowing local Norwegians became concerned about what they were witnessing. The Germans became aware of the concerns and that was the end of the mission, which to a large extent, the success of which had always been dependent on the element surprise.

In the final year of the war, Kayser was tasked with establishing bases in some of the more remote areas of Norway to provide a safe haven for Norwegians who were on the run from German forces, regardless of whether that was the army or the Gestapo. It was also hoped that besides providing a safe haven, some of those who were looked after would be happy to be trained in guerrilla tactics, hence making them useful additions to the Norwegian resistance movement.

Kayser was the second in command of the base at Bjorn West in Masfjorden. He arrived there in October 1944 along with fellow Kompani Linge member, Severin Synnes. They had made their way across the North Sea on the submarine chaser vessel M/S *Vigra*, which was one of three that had been donated to the Shetland Bus operation by the USA to replace the older and much slower Norwegian fishing vessels that had made up the Shetland Bus until October 1943.

For his wartime exploits Kayser was deservedly awarded a total of fourteen decorations from a number of grateful nations including Norway, the UK and the USA.

Arne Kjelstrup was a soldier in the Norwegian army when Germany invaded Norway in April 1940. During the fighting he was shot by a German bullet, but prior to entering his body the bullet hit a pair of wire cutters he was holding, greatly reducing the velocity at which it struck him. It was deemed too dangerous to try and remove the bullet from where it had lodged, and it remained inside him for the rest of his life.

When it came time for the Norwegian army to surrender, Kjelstrup did not fancy becoming a prisoner of war, so like many of his compatriots he decided to make his way to neighbouring Sweden. His final destination was the UK, a location which he must have been extremely determined to reach, as his must have been one of the longest journeys anybody made throughout the entire Second World War to get to the UK. After leaving Sweden he made his way to Russia, travelling via Moscow and the port of Odessa. From there he made his way to Istanbul in Turkey, then through the Suez Canal, before arriving in Durban, South Africa, on to Cape Town, before crossing the Atlantic Ocean to Trinidad in the Caribbean. He then sailed to Halifax in Nova Scotia, then back across the Atlantic Ocean to Liverpool before making his way down to London.

In the capital he enlisted in the Kompani Linge. On 18 October 1942, he was one of the Grouse team parachuted on to the Hardangervidda plateau. He was then involved in Operation Gunnerside, mentioned in some detail earlier in this chapter in relation to Knut Haugland and Claus Helberg.

After the successful mission at Vemork and the destruction of the heavy water equipment, Kjelstrup remained in Norway and assisted the Milorg resistance movement. He later returned to the UK where he underwent further training which focused on sabotage. On 5 October 1944, he was sent back to Norway as part of Operation Sunshine, an anti-demolition mission which continued until the end of the war. The belief was that occupying German forces would operate a scorched earth policy of destroying as much of the Norwegian industrial infrastructure as they could before the war came to an end, once they knew it was a lost cause.

There were four major power plants in Eastern Norway alone, and if the Germans managed to destroy them, it would account for some 60 per cent of the required energy supplies for that region of the country. That was simply not something that could be allowed to happen.

Kjelstrup was in charge of the team that had been allocated to prevent the Nore Power Station from being blown up by the retreating Germans. They were given the code name of Operation Starlight. The group's wireless operator was Eldar Hagen, and by the end of the war, Kjelstrup had hundreds of fighting men at his disposal, should they be needed to be called upon.

Reidar Kvaal escaped to the UK in 1940 after Norway had fallen to the Germans, on one of the Norwegian fishing boats which would go on to become part of the Shetland Bus operation. Once on British soil he enlisted in the Kompani Linge and undertook training which would see him eventually sent back to Norway to carry out operations in German-occupied territory. His chance came in 1943 when, in charge of Operation Lapwing, he led a team of commandos who were parachuted into the Haltdalen Mountains.

His military career continued after the war and he went on to reach the rank of lieutenant general in the Norwegian army. He lived to the ripe old age of 100 years and 4 months.

Johannes Kvittingen, although not widely known, played an important role in the Second World War. Before the war, he was a Norwegian microbiologist and chief physician in Trondheim and worked at the Bacterial Laboratory of the Norwegian Armed

Forces. After the German invasion and occupation of Norway, the laboratory closed down and Kvittingen made his way to the UK on a Norwegian fishing vessel, eventually arriving in London, where he worked with medicinal services for Norwegians who were in exile throughout the UK.

Prior to leaving Norway he had saved four British soldiers who had become lost and disorientated in the vastness of the Norwegian mountains. This act alone had brought him to the attention of the British authorities, who were quick to both recognise and appreciate his vast array of skills and attributes. In the latter months of 1940, he was asked by the British military authorities to head up the recruiting team of Norwegians who had been identified as being potential Norwegian agents for Britain's SOE.

This was no easy task. There were hundreds of Norwegians who had escaped their German-occupied nation by making their way across the North Sea in relatively small fishing boats. After arriving in the UK they then declared their desire to return to Norway to fight against the German occupying forces. One of the issues for Kvittingen and his team was not only to determine who would make a good agent, but who was possibly a Norwegian collaborator with the Germans who had simply made his way to the UK to infiltrate the very groups whose role it was to return to Norway to cause disruption to the occupying forces.

Norman Lind was already living in the UK, where he undertook his higher education, at the beginning of the Second World War. Initially he enlisted in the British army as a sapper in the Royal Engineers, before spending the following two years training to become an officer.

Eventually, and almost inevitably for a young, determined Norwegian, he ended up becoming part of the Kompani Linge. He was one of those sent to Norway in 1944 as part of Operation Sunshine, and was also one of those responsible for putting the operation together.

Martin Linge and the part he played in the Second World War for his native Norway has been widely reported on. Before the outbreak of the war he had been a reservist in the Norwegian army and when British forces landed at Andalsnes, in what for them would ultimately lead to defeat, Linge worked as a liaison officer between the Norwegian and British forces. Early on in the fighting Linge was wounded during the German bombing of a makeshift airfield at Setnesmoen; his injuries were sufficiently bad for him to be sent to the UK by boat to have his wounds attended to. This made him the first wounded Norwegian soldier to arrive in the UK.

Having recovered from his wounds, he (along with Nordhal Grieg and Olav Rytter) was the first to come up with the idea of waging guerrilla-style warfare against the German occupation of their country. It was an idea that appealed to those at the War Office. In August 1940, the recruiting for what was to become the Kompani Linge began. But by agreeing to this, Linge had not given up on being a soldier and was determined to become one of those involved in the very same operations that he was recruiting men to be part of.

Erling Sven Lorentzen, who went on to become a post-war Norwegian shipowner and industrialist, as well as a billionaire, served with the Kompani Linge as a radio operator during the Second World War. In 1953 he married the eldest child of King Olav V of Norway, Princess Ragnhild.

Maximo Guillermo 'Max' Manus is remembered for being one of the best saboteurs of the Second World War. His original family surname was Magnussen, but his father, Johan, changed his name to Juan Manus after having lived in a number of foreign countries for several years where the main language spoken was Spanish.

During the Soviet-Finnish Winter War 1939–1940, he was a volunteer fighter for Finland and only returned to Norway on 9 April 1940, the day of the German invasion of his country. He was an early member of the Norwegian resistance movement and was captured and interrogated by the Gestapo in 1941. Miraculously, he managed to escape but was injured in the process and had to be treated in hospital in Oslo for minor injuries of bruising and a mild concussion. But when Gestapo officers made enquiries about his condition, the doctors bravely lied and told them that he had broken his back, had a serious concussion, and would need to stay in hospital for weeks if not months. After being in the hospital for nearly a month, he escaped via a second storey window with the aid of a rope which had been provided by one of his nurses.

He made his way to Sweden, travelled through the Soviet Union and Turkey before taking a ship from Arabia to Cape Town in South Africa, and continued on to America. There he joined the Norwegian army and underwent training in Canada before crossing the Atlantic to Scotland, where he learned about sabotage work. Once his training was complete, he and a number of others were parachuted into Norway, landing in the forests near Oslo.

In Norway he became involved in numerous sabotage attempts on the German ships at anchor in the Oslofjord. He used homemade limpet mines and what were known as 'swimmer assisted torpedoes', with mixed success. To acquire the parts he needed for his weapons and also to relax, he crossed back and forth into neighbouring Sweden. A number of those who he had arrived with in Norway were not so fortunate. They were captured, tortured and killed, but Manus always managed to escape, sometimes only by the skin of his teeth. He went on to become an expert in sabotaging ships with limpet mines and was responsible for the destruction of a number of Kriegsmarine vessels including the SS *Donau* on 16 January 1945.

The *Donau* was a German vessel built as a refrigerated cargo vessel in Hamburg in 1929. At the outbreak of the Second World War, she was requisitioned by the Kreigsmarine (German navy) and was equipped with anti-aircraft guns and depth charges.

The relevance of the *Donau* was that she became known as the 'slave ship' after the SS and the Gestapo transported 540 Jews from Norway to Stettin in Germany, and from there by train to Auschwitz. Only nine of those deportees survived. Their journey had begun when they were handed over by Norwegian police to members of the SS at Pier 1 in Oslo harbour on 26 November 1942.

Manus's wartime work saw him awarded the DSO, the Military Cross with Bar, along with the Medal of Norwegian Volunteers to Finland, the War Cross with two Swords, the Defence Medal 1940–1945, the Haakon VII 70th Anniversary Medal, His Majesty the King's Commemorative Medal 1940–1945, Winter War Medal with 'Lappi' Clasp, the American award of the Medal of Freedom with Silver Palm.

After the war, Manus paid for his wartime bravery. He had nightmares, suffered from alcoholism and experienced bouts of depression, some of which he talked about in interviews.

Later in life, he and his wife, Tikken Lindbraekke, whom he married in 1947, moved to Spain where he died in 1996 at the age of 81.

Svein Øvergaard was a well-known musician and band leader before the war, and as if by way of showing how versatile he was, in 1938 he became the junior light heavyweight boxing champion of Norway.

Finn Palmstrøm was a solicitor and a deputy judge before the Second World War; the only kind of fighting that he knew of was the verbal kind that went on in a courtroom.

However, in the Winter War of 1939–1940, between Finland and the Soviet Union, Palmstrøm fought as a volunteer on the Finnish side. No sooner had the fighting there finished than he returned to Norway to find that his country had just been invaded by German forces, where he once again fought against an oppressive nation. After Germany's victory, rather than risk being executed as a resistance fighter, he made his escape by fishing boat to Scotland. He enlisted in the Kompani Linge and underwent his initial training throughout 1941 and 1942, being sent back to Norway to take part in a number of operations.

In 1944, he was set the task of being in charge of the Norwegian National Office, which had been set up by the Norwegian government in exile to register people who it regarded as war criminals for crimes committed on Norwegian soil during the wartime German occupation of Norway.

In 1945 he became an acting assistant secretary in the Norwegian Ministry of Justice and was present at the Nuremberg Trials throughout the latter part of 1945 and 1946. Along with fellow Norwegian Rolf Normann Torgersen, he was responsible for writing the report on Germany's war crimes against Norway.

Alv Kristian Pedersen was a member of the Kompani Linge. After the war he was awarded the Most Excellent Order of the British Empire by the British government.

Jens-Anton Poulsson became a lieutenant in the Kompani Linge during the Second World War and was the leader of the Grouse team, which parachuted into Norway on 18 October 1942 on the Hardangervidda plateau. He was one of those who saw success at Vemork in February 1943. After returning to Scotland in early 1943, he was at the training centre in Nethy Bridge when he was presented with the Norwegian award of St Olav's Medal with Oak Branch by King Haakon, who was in exile in the UK.

He returned to Norway on 5 October 1944 as part of Operation Sunshine. He survived the war and remained in the Norwegian army until 1982, when he was 62, by which time he had reached the rank of colonel.

Einar Riis was one of the many young Norwegians who enlisted in the Norwegian resistance movement, fully embracing all the dangers which went with it. In 1943 he was involved in Operation Mardonis, which involved the sinking of German shipping in Oslo harbour, working alongside agents of the British SOE.

As the war continued so things became more difficult for Riis. As an active member of the Norwegian resistance, he never knew if one morning he would be woken up by jack-booted Nazis kicking down his front door, or whether somebody who he believed to be his friend and fellow resistance worker was in fact a German collaborator. With this in mind he decided that he had to leave his beloved Norway behind. His choice of destination was Canada, and he had decided he wanted to become a pilot in the Royal Norwegian Air Force, so he made his way to their training camp in southern Ontario, which was also known as Little Norway.

He survived the war, but afterwards moved first to France and then to Italy, and worked as a shipping broker as well as in the aviation business, eventually setting up his own aviation company with three Douglas DC-3 aircraft.

Boy Rist was, at 28 years old, far from being a boy when Germany invaded Norway in April 1940. He had served in the Norwegian navy from October 1939, on board the *Heimdal,* a 47-year-old Norwegian warship, which had been mobilised to safeguard Norwegian neutrality at sea.

Rist took part in the fighting against the Germans in northern Norway, but on 6 June 1940, just four days before Norwegian forces capitulated, he left Norway via Tromsø and made his way across the North Sea in a small fishing boat, the forerunner of the Shetland Bus. His naval experience was of great use to the British, who sent him to work at the Rosyth Naval Station in Scotland.

In May 1943, he transferred to working as part of the Motor Boat Flotilla unit based in Shetland, before becoming part of the crew of the corvette *Eglantine*, which was part of the Royal Norwegian Navy. In June 1944, he also took part in the Normandy landings.

Joachim Rønneberg was another who escaped from Norway by fishing boat across the North Sea to Shetland. Once in Scotland he joined Kompani Linge as a second lieutenant. He was not only part of, but led, the six-man Operation Gunnerside team, which was involved in the successful February 1943 raid on the Norsk Hydro heavy water production plant in Vemork. The Germans did not immediately realise the plant had been attacked, but when they did, they sent nearly 3,000 men to look for those responsible.

Rønneberg and his five men escaped to Sweden, via an arduous fourteen-day march through strength-sapping, and at times, knee-deep snow; a distance of some 250 miles. An incredible feat of endurance when compared to the 1991 escape by 22 Special Air Service Corporal, Colin Armstrong, holder of the Military Medal, who was better known by his pseudonym of Chris Ryan. He claimed to have escaped on foot to Syria, covering a distance of 180 miles.

The six members of the raiding party came up with a different means of escape. They stayed in Norway moving around and stayed at different locations until the Germans simply gave up looking for them.

Rønneberg was involved in other wartime missions in German-occupied Norway, including the January 1945 mission to destroy the railway bridge which crosses over the River Rauma, just north of Stuguflat. He and his three-man team managed to blow up the bridge with a large charge of plastic explosives, but just three weeks later the Germans had repaired the bridge, and normal service was quickly resumed.

For his wartime military service, Rønneberg received awards from Norway, Britain, America and France.

Bjørn Rørholt was a cadet at the Norwegian Military Academy and was involved in the early fighting to save his nation from defeat at the hands of the Germans. When the battle was over, Rørholt initially became a prisoner of war, but it was not long before he was released and he returned to his pre-war studies at the Norwegian Institute of Technology.

Sometime during 1941, Rørholt became involved with the Norwegian intelligence movement, and specifically a part of the two radio communications stations which had been set up by Britain's Secret Intelligence Service, one of which was in Oslo and the other in Trondheim. These radio stations allowed the Norwegian resistance movement to have direct contact with London, providing them with up-to-date information, such as troop movements, as soon as it became available.

In September 1941, the Germans discovered the location of the Trondheim site, and Rørholt was fortunate to escape capture. He travelled to England via Sweden, only to discover that the British authorities were concerned about using him operationally again for fear that the Germans might well be aware of his physical appearance. But eventually he had his chance.

It was well known that the German battleship *Tirpitz* was holed up in a Norwegian fjord. The problem for the allies was, if she ventured out into the Atlantic Ocean, her presence could be catastrophic for Allied shipping. In the latter part of 1942, Rørholt was sent back to Norway on a vessel of the Shetland Bus, with a cover story that he was an insurance agent who needed to travel around to visit his clients; the reality was that he was sent back to Norway to operate a radio station, code named Lerkin, which had been set up by the Secret Intelligence Service. The system consisted of four separate radio transmitters in the Trondheim area.

After a return to the UK in 1942, where he worked for a while in a training capacity teaching the next generation of Norwegian radio transmitters, he return to Norway to conduct further missions in 1944, and was still there when the Germans surrendered in May 1945.

Harald Sandvik became a teacher in Norwegian secondary education in 1941, by which time he was already leading a double life by working for the Norwegian resistance movement. As was the case of many of his compatriots who were involved in similar activities, he had to flee the country to avoid being arrested by the Gestapo.

These were unprecedented times and what previously had been normality, changed beyond all comprehension. It was not just the Gestapo and the German authorities that members of the resistance had to consider: from June 1940 onwards, those Norwegians who had chosen to become collaborators with the Germans, either for financial gain or ideological reasons, became a real and present danger for them.

Sandvik's story is a slightly strange one. Prior to and during the occupation of Norway by German forces, he had been studying at the University of Oslo, where he took and passed an academic degree in Arts and Letters in 1940, and another the following year in teaching.

His involvement with the Norwegian resistance movement meant he then had to leave Norway. Having safely reached Sweden, he became head of the Sports Office at the Norwegian Legation in Stockholm in 1942, the same year that he married. The next that is known about Sandvik is he was in the UK, specifically in Scotland, where he was in charge of Kompani Linge of the SOE, and running the physical education programme at No. 26 special training school.

His time in Scotland, in the capacity he was in, would have meant that he undoubtedly had involvement with the Shetland Bus because he would have used its boats to transfer some of his agents to and from Norway. He would have also been extremely interested in Norwegian refugees who arrived in Shetland from Norway to see if they were suitable to be trained as agents of Kompani Linge.

Einnar Skinnarland was a member of the Norwegian resistance movement, and was awarded the Distinguished Conduct Medal (DCM) by the British government.

Gunnar Fridtjof Thurmann Sønsteby was a member of the Norwegian resistance movement. He was also known by the nickname 'Kjakan' which in English means 'The Cheeks'. He was the most highly decorated Norwegian citizen of the Second World War, and the only Norwegian to have been awarded the War Cross with three swords, Norway's highest military award.

When the Germans invaded Norway, Sønsteby was working as an accountant, but after the country's regular armed forces were ordered to surrender by their government he enlisted in the Norwegian resistance forces in Ostlandet, and was also involved in the underground press.

In 1941 he became a member of the SOE (where he was officially known as 'Agent 24'). In 1942, having travelled across the North Sea in a vessel of the Shetland Bus to Norway, he made his way to Sweden on an assignment, but whilst there he was arrested by the Swedish police and imprisoned for three months, after which he managed to convince them that he was not the same Gunnar Sønsteby that they were looking for, and he was released.

By 1943, he was back in Norway, still working undercover as an SOE agent, when he was arrested by the Gestapo, but before he could be interrogated he managed to escape, and made his way back to Sweden before returning to the UK.

In June 1943, he enlisted in the Kompani Linge, and after completing his training in October 1943, was parachuted into Norway to help train, organise, instruct and lead the Norwegian resistance movement. Initially he became the leader of the Milorg group, and later the same month he became the head of the newly formed Oslo Gang, most of whom were members of Kompani Linge, and whose main purpose was sabotage. Others in the group included Andreas Aubert, Viggo Axelsen, Gregers Gram, Henrik Hop, William Houlder, Max Manus, Martin Olsen, Arthur Pevik, Birger Rasmussen, Tor Stenersen, and Edward Tallaksen. Individually and collectively, they were an impressive group of men, and extremely good at what they did.

They were a daring group, who, despite the obvious dangers of what they were involved in, carried on regardless, in the knowledge that there was a much bigger machine in which they were just a small cog. One of their acts of sabotage was an attack on the Norwegian Central Bank, where they stole the master plates for the printing of Norwegian paper currency, which were then smuggled out of the country and handed to representatives of the exiled Norwegian government in London.

Their acts of sabotage were never random; there was always a reason behind what they did. The Germans had started collating the names of young Norwegian men with a view to recruiting as many of them as possible and sending them to fight on the Eastern Front as part of the Germanic SS. The details of these young men were held in the office of the Norwegian Forced Labour department in Oslo. To thwart the Nazis efforts, Sønsteby and his men blew up the office where these records were kept, destroying the relevant files in the process, and sparing a large number of young Norwegian men from having to go off and fight for the Nazis.

In September 1944, Sønsteby and his men also carried out a raid on the Kongsberg Munitions Factory, which resulted in the destruction of a large quantity of guns and many of the machine tools which were used to make the guns.

On 8 February 1945, the head of the National Mobile Police Service in Norway, Karl Marthinsen, was shot dead in a burst of machine-gun fire by Sønsteby's group whilst he was being driven near his home in Oslo. He had been in his position since 1940 and had a poor reputation amongst the Norwegian population. Part of his job saw him having to liaise between the Norwegian police, the Quisling regime and the Gestapo, a role which he greatly enjoyed. He was the man ultimately responsible for the deportation of Jews from Norway to Auschwitz, and the mistreatment of many more. He was a callous and cowardly individual who took full advantage of his position. His sadistic side was quite apparent and was clearly shown by his encouragement of the tactic of torture by his men.

The enthusiasm by Sønsteby and his men to continually harass their German occupiers, never waned. When the Nazis threatened an increase in the number of foods that were to be rationed, they responded by stealing 75,000 ration books, stopping the plan from being put into place. They managed to damage a large number of German aircraft in Kosvoll, and destroyed an oil storage depot in Oslo harbour, which resulted in the loss of large quantities of much-needed lubricating oil for the German war effort.

Aware of the state of the war elsewhere in Europe, Sønsteby decided on a plan of blowing up the railway lines of major routes after the D-Day landings in Normandy, in order to prevent the Germans from sending any of their men stationed in Norway to support their colleagues who were trying to hold back the Allied advances throughout German-occupied France.

The Gestapo only found out Sønsteby's real identity right at the end of the war, and too late for his arrest or execution to make any real difference to the outcome of the war. The big advantage he had was his appearance, which was really quite unremarkable, and nothing like what might be imagined of a man who was in charge of such a successful and celebrated group of men. He was a very resourceful and intuitive individual, who had become at one with his very existence, so much so that it had become second nature to him. What others might have viewed as skilful and remarkable, to him was just everyday life. He also rarely spent more than a few days at a time living in a place, moving from one home to another as and when it felt right to do so. Whatever it was that he had, whether it was intuition, foresight, information or just good old-fashioned luck, it kept him alive.

Sønsteby was once described as having 'nerves of steel', a description he did not readily agree with. The way he saw himself was somebody who was emotionless, a cold individual, traits which allowed him remain cool under pressure and often stopped him from over-reacting, although he did admit to begin feeling anxious towards the end of the war, to such an extent that he took to carrying a hand grenade with him everywhere he went during the last few months, knowing full well that if he was ever captured by the Gestapo, their treatment of him would not be at all pleasant.

One regret that Sønsteby did have, was that because of his actions his father was detained by the Gestapo and held in custody between February 1943 and December 1944, but he too survived the war.

After the war, Sønsteby turned down numerous job offers both in Norway and abroad, most of which came from intelligence agencies. He had seen and done many things during the course of the war and had certainly had enough of fighting and everything that went with it. Instead, he moved to America where he lived a more sedate way of life, although he did give many lectures about the war and his part in it.

At one such lecture he said what could be seen one of the most poignant things ever written about history.

'As long as I live, I will tell the important facts. The historians can analyse, but I was there.'

Inge Steensland was a member and leader of the Norwegian resistance movement. He went on to become a member of Kompani Linge, and was backwards and forwards across the North Sea involved in a number of wartime missions in German-occupied Norway. In June 1944, he was also involved in the invasion of Normandy. For his wartime service he was awarded the Norwegian War Medal, the Defence Medal 1940–1945, as well as Britain's DSO.

Hans Storhaug fought against the Germans as a soldier in the Norwegian army, specifically at Solor and Dovre. He managed to stay at large after Germany's victory by discarding his uniform and pretending to be a civilian, but fearing he would eventually be captured by the German authorities, he found himself a passage on a local fishing boat and escaped from the municipality of Alesund in December 1940, arriving in Shetland the following day. This was on the same route that the Shetland Bus would take, on the same type of vessel.

On his arrival in Scotland he enlisted in the Kompani Linge. Having successfully completed his training, he was sent back to Norway as part of Operation Anklet which took place on Boxing

Day 1941. He was also part of the Gunnerside team who took part in the raid on the heavy water plant at Vemork in February 1943. In October 1943, he was part of Operation Glebe that saw six men parachuted into Norway. Three of them died almost immediately after landing when they came down in a lake where the water was lightly frozen. Being in such a situation, heavily weighed down with all their clothes and equipment, with their parachutes still attached, their fates were sadly sealed. Storhaug and his two colleagues who survived the landings made their way to Sweden, where they remained until March 1944, before returning to Norway and the area of Osterdalen, remaining there until the end of the war.

Birger Edvin Martin Strømsheim was a building contractor by profession, work that he was still engaged in during and after the time of the German invasion of Norway. Sometime during 1941, the exact date of which is unclear, Strømsheim and his wife Aase, decided that a life under Nazi occupation was not for them, with Strømsheim determined to do his bit in ridding his beloved Norway of the oppression of Nazi rule.

They found passage on one of the many fishing boats that were more than willing to take Norwegian refugees across the potentially perilous waters of the North Sea and to freedom in the UK. Once there he enlisted with Kompani Linge and began the training that, when completed, would see him return to Norway as a saboteur.

In February 1943, the well-respected Strømsheim was part of the successful Operation Gunnerside team parachuted back into Norway, landing at Telemark. After returning to Scotland, he was awarded the St Olav's Medal with Oak Branch, in a ceremony at Nethy Bridge. The medal, which is awarded for 'exceptional services to Norway during time of war', was presented to him by King Haakon of Norway.

What the men of Operation Gunnerside achieved in sabotaging the heavy water plant at Vemork, was later claimed by the SOE to have been the most successful act of sabotage of the entire Second

World War. I dare say that in certain military quarters, that claim might well be disputed.

In April 1944, Strømsheim returned to Norway as part of Operation Fieldfare. Along with Joachim Rønneberg and Olav Aarsæther, Strømsheim built a log cabin in the remote area of Sunnmore. Its purpose was for it to be their base and home whilst they carried out acts of sabotage against the German supply lines running through the valley of Romsdal. The location chosen for the cabin could not have been better as it was situated under a natural overhanging rock face, which provided it with excellent protection from discovery by German aircraft.

Strømsheim who survived the war, died on 10 November 2012 in Oslo. He was 101 years old.

John Sveinsson's post-war life has been recorded in more detail than his wartime exploits. Wanting to do more in the fight against Nazi Germany's occupation of his country, he left Norway in 1941, with his initial destination being Sweden. By 1943, he had reached Scotland where he enlisted in the Kompani Linge and underwent military training, which included parachuting and sabotage techniques, but it would not be until the latter stages of the war in early 1945 that he would see active service on his return to Norway.

Whilst in Scotland he played for Dundee United Football Club. In October 1945, he played for SFK Lyn in the Norwegian Football Cup Final against Fredrikstad. After a 1-1 draw at the Ullevaal stadium in Oslo before a crowd of 34,162, on 14 October 1945, there was a replay two weeks later, which also ended in a 1-1 draw after extra time. One week later, in the second replay, SFK Lyn secured a resounding 4-0 victory. Sveinsson went on to represent Norway on three occasions, scoring once.

A member of the Fredrikstad team in that final, Reidar Brede Olsen, had also served as a member of the Milorg resistance movement during the Second World War.

Gunnar Bryde Syverstad arrived in the UK in February 1944, possibly on one of the boats used by the Shetland Bus. He then became a member of the SOE's Kompani Linge. He was parachuted back into Norway as part of Operation Sunshine, which ran between October 1944 and the end of the war. It was a mission to protect and prevent essential Norwegian installations and industry, in particular large power stations such as the one at Vemork, from being destroyed in a scorched earth action by German forces as the war drew to an end.

Before Germany's invasion and occupation of Norway, Syverstad had worked at the Vemork hydroelectric power plant as a laboratory assistant.

Edvard Tallaksen was an army reservist at the time of the German invasion of his country, having completed his obligatory military service in 1936. He was involved in the fighting in southern Norway, but when Germany caused Norwegian forces to surrender in June 1940, Tallaksen had no intention of becoming a prisoner of war. Along with five others he took a boat across the North Sea to Shetland and enlisted in the Kompani Linge.

During the summer months of 1944, Tallaksen took part in a number of sabotage missions with the Milorg resistance group. On Monday, 13 November 1944, Tallaksen and Gregers Gram, a second lieutenant in Kompani Linge, supposedly went to meet with a group of German deserters at a café in Oslo. But it was a trap. In the subsequent shoot-out Gram was killed and Tallaksen was shot in the jaw. He spent the next two weeks in Solo's Aker Hospital, before he was transferred to Akershus Fortress.

Knowing full well that the only reason the Gestapo had been so interested in his wellbeing and recovery was so that they could get him to tell them everything he knew about the Norwegian resistance movement, he committed suicide in the Fortress on 29 November 1944, rather than risk betraying any of his comrades.

Gunvald Tomstad was an extremely interesting character. Immediately before the invasion and occupation of Norway, he worked as a typographer for the *Agder* newspaper, which was based in Flekkefjord and had first been published on 25 April 1877. With the German occupation came the closure of the newspaper and Tomstad suddenly found himself out of a job.

He was approached and recruited by agents of the British Secret Intelligence Service, with the purpose of monitoring the Norwegian coast for German naval activity. The team of agents was also tasked with making contact with Niels Henrik David Bohr and his colleagues, who it was believed were 'working' on a German atom bomb project.

As Tomstad had his own handmade radio transmitter set, it was he who was nominated to be the direct contact between the group and London. In 1941, he had joined the Norwegian fascist party, Nasjonal Samling, the paramilitary quite often referred to as NS; not because he had turned on his own people, but because he had been asked to by his British masters to do so.

Initially everything went well, and for two years he was able to freely transmit messages back to England about all kinds of German military-related developments. But all his friends and neighbours saw him as was a high-ranking member of the Nasjonal Samling Party, which was greatly disliked by many Norwegians.

In an effort to locate and capture illegal radio transmitters and those who owned them, he worked with German counter intelligence, but purely to pre-warn those individuals concerned so that they could escape or get rid of their sets before the German authorities came knocking.

As a young member of the Nasjonal Samling Party, he would have been expected to 'volunteer' to serve in the Waffen SS 'Divison Viking' on the Russian Front, not a location that most blue-eyed, blonde-haired, fully paid up members of the Nazi Party ever wanted to be sent to. To avoid this experience he broke his leg in a motorbike accident; the break was so bad that it prevented him from having to undergo military service for the Germans.

His cover was nearly blown when he attempted to aid a number of Norwegian SOE members who had been involved in a crash landing when their aircraft came down in the south of Norway on their way to carry out a sabotage mission. In attempting to help them, he was nearly captured by German troops but managed to escape by making his way on foot through the mountain passes during an unforgiving Norwegian winter. He made it to Sweden, but only just, as his health was deteriorating rapidly due to hypothermia and utter exhaustion. From there he was airlifted back to the UK, and in essence that was his war over with, but not out of choice. His health and fitness were simply no longer up to the standard needed.

He underwent further training once he had fully recovered from his escape to Sweden, but his broken leg, exhaustion and the stress of having lived a double life for two years had taken its toll on him physically and mentally, and he was still only 25 years old. After the war his health gradually declined over a number of years. He died in 1970 of a perforated gastric ulcer, aged 51.

It is sad to think that a young man like Tomstad spent two years working for the Allies in Norway, whilst the very people he was ultimately trying to save and help believed that he was a Nazi collaborator and he was unable to say anything to anyone to make them think otherwise. The stress and pressure he was under must have had an enormous strain on his wellbeing.

Leif Hans Larsen Tronstad, a graduate of the Norwegian Institute of Technology in 1927, returned there in 1936 as a Professor of Chemistry, and was one of the very first people involved in heavy water research. In 1941, he left Norway for the UK and in 1943 was one of the architects of Operation Gunnerside, which lead to the successful raid on the heavy water power station at Vemork.

Despite his desire to return to Norway so that he could be involved in a more hands-on manner, he was refused permission to do so by Norwegian military authorities in the UK. He eventually got his wish when he was parachuted into Norway on 4 October 1944, as part of Operation Sunshine.

In March 1945, Tronstad and his group became aware that the Nazi-installed bailiff of the mountain village of Rauland, Torgeir Lognvik, was becoming suspicious of reports of comings and goings in the area of their cabin. So a plan was devised to deal with the situation. On 11 March 1945, Jon Landsverk, a member of the Norwegian resistance movement, persuaded the bailiff to go with him to the area of the cabin on the pretext of showing him some stolen goods he had discovered. During their journey they were met by Gunnar Syverstad and Einar Skinnarland, who took Lognvik prisoner and led him to a different cabin, high up in the hills over Syerbekkstolen. There he was tied up and interrogated by Landsverk, Syverstad and Tronstad. Unbeknown to everybody, including Lognvik, his brother Johans was suspicious of the meeting and had followed on behind at a safe distance. Simply following the ski tracks in the fresh snow took him right to where his brother was being interrogated. Tronstad and his men had made three fatal mistakes. Firstly, they had made absolutely no effort to cover or confuse their tracks, which admittedly was difficult to achieve in the circumstances. Secondly, once they had reached the cabin at Syerbekkstolen, they had not deemed it necessary to leave any kind of guard outside, either covertly or overtly. Such a basic mistake, but also a very costly one. Thirdly, they had sat Lognivk down, but had not secured him to a chair or a table.

On reaching the cabin, Johans Lognvik kicked the front door in, taking everybody by surprise. Opening fire he shot and killed Gunnar Syverstad. It would appear that some of the resistance men were either not armed, which seems highly unlikely, or did not have their weapons to hand. Such reasoning is because rather than shooting Johans Lognivik, Tronstad rushed at him, trying to wrestle the gun from his hands, but was shot dead in the process.

The Lognivik brothers then managed to escape. Jon Landsverk and Einar Skinnarland survived and disposed of the bodies of their dead colleagues in a nearby lake, but they were discovered the following day by German troops, and burnt.

On 30 May 1945, just three weeks after the end of the war and of German rule in their country, Tronstad's remains were given a funeral with full military honours at the Vestre gravlund cemetery in Oslo. For his wartime bravery, he was awarded the War Cross with Sword, Norway's highest decoration for military gallantry, the Norwegian War Medal and the Defence Medal 1940–1945. Great Britain added the Order of the British Empire (OBE) and the DSO. America awarded him the United States Medal of Freedom with Bronze Palm, whilst the French awarded him the Chevalier of the French Legion d'honneur and the Croix de Guerre.

Johans Lognvik was put on trial after the war, as part of a purge on those who were found guilty of the murder of both Gunnar Syverstad and Leif Tronstad, whilst Torgeir Lognvik was charged and convicted of one count of attempted murder as it was suggested that after Johans had shot Tronstad, Torgeir had finished him off with a rifle butt to the head.

The aftermath of these events is very interesting, as an inference could be taken that Torgeir, who had been given the position of bailiff in Rauland by the Nazis, had been given such a role because they believed he was in agreement with their way of doing things.

Both Torgeir and Johans Lognvik remained in Rauland after the war, and spent the rest of their lives there. Johans died on 12 December 1991 at the age of 95, and Torgeir died on 27 June 1994 at the age of 86. Both men were also buried in the village of Rauland. In the circumstances, it can only be assumed that there was little in the way of any animosity towards either of the brothers after the events of March 1945 that resulted in the deaths of Gunnar Syverstad and Leif Tronstad.

Ragnar Ulstein was a writer and journalist before the Second World War, and during it he was a member of the Norwegian resistance movement. After the war he wrote numerous books about it, including one about volunteers sailing from Norway to Scotland, and another about refugee traffic from Norway to Sweden.

By the time Germany had forced Norway into surrendering in June 1940, Ulstein was just finishing his secondary education in Volda. He had no intention of sitting round, waiting to find out what life was going to be like under Nazi rule, so later the same year he found a captain of a boat on the west coast of Norway who was prepared to give him passage to the UK. It was because of such journeys that the very idea came about for the Shetland Bus.

Having arrived in Shetland he enlisted with Kompani Linge. He first returned to Norway in December 1941, as part of Operation Anklet, the large commando raid in the Lofoten Islands. He returned to the UK soon after the raid. In 1943 he once again returned to Norway as part of Operation Vestige I, which was a raid on German shipping in Svelgen harbour, where a timed limpet mine was placed on the hull of a ship. The mine was supposed to have been timed to go off some hours later, by which time she would have been under way and already out of the harbour. But it exploded too early when the vessel was still at anchor. The explosion caused her to run aground rather than sink. After the mission, Ulstein returned to the UK.

In 1944, Ulstein was once again sent back to Norway, this time by way of a vessel of the Shetland Bus operation. On this occasion his mission was not to take part in a raid but to train and teach members of the Milorg resistance group, who were situated in Soqn of Fjordane, then a county in western Norway. He was dropped off with another man, Harald Svindseth, near the town of Floro.

Between them they set up a further two Milorg groups. Ulstein set up one in Fosskamben, with the code name of *Siskin*, whilst Svindseth began his group at the village of Svelgen, giving his the code name of *Snowflake*.

Being involved in such activities brought with it many dangers. Knowing who could be trusted was a major issue for a start. Not all of those who would provide the German authorities with information about local matters were collaborators, some were just afraid about what might happen to them and their families if they did not pass on what they knew.

Olav Rise was a local man and a member of the *Siskin* group, which at the time was at Sogndalsdalen. He was arrested in February 1945, although Ragnar Ulstein managed to escape. Word reached the villagers at Fosskamben that German forces were on their way. This provided the men of the *Siskin* group not only time to escape, but sufficient time to move a weapons and ammunition cache that had been hidden in the village. If that had been discovered, the chances are that all of the villagers would have been killed and their properties set on fire.

Why the Germans made their way to Fosskamben and what they had been told about the village is unclear, although the chances of it having been a random visit were extremely unlikely. However, this was not something that made men such as Ulstein quit; he wasn't that kind of man. He simply moved location, regrouped, and went again. He met Heiberg and Knagenhjelm at the picturesque village of Fjaerland in the municipality of Sogndal, and set up another base at the village of Fronningen. In no time at all this new group had a network of nearly 500 people, but it did not exist for too long because on 8 May 1945, the Germans surrendered and Norway was once again a free nation.

Ulstein and a section of his group assisted in the decommissioning of German forces in the areas close to where he was.

For his wartime efforts Ulstein was awarded the St Olav's Medal with two oak branches, the Defence Medal 1940–1945, and the Haakon VII 70th Anniversary Medal. Britain also awarded him the Military Medal.

Once the war was over, Ulstein still had a role to play. He was involved in the Independent Norwegian Brigade Group in

Germany, which was a Norwegian expeditionary force stationed in the British Zone of Occupation in Germany. This continued for seven years between 1946 and 1953; the first two years saw them based in Hanover, and from 1948 their base moved to the Schleswig Holstein region of Germany.

After finally returning to Norway, his new world was as a journalist and a writer, being involved with numerous newspapers and writing several books.

Erling Welle-Strand was a student at the University of Oslo at the time of the German invasion. Not surprisingly, this curtailed his studies for the immediate future. He quickly took up arms against the Germans as part of the Norwegian resistance movement, and was involved in fighting at Valdres and Bagn.

After Germany was victorious in June 1940, Welle-Strand went to ground to avoid capture and possible execution by the Germans. Feeling that he had no other option, especially if he wanted to continue the fight against the Germans, in 1941, along with friends Reidar Kvinge and Per Hysing-Dahl, he escaped in a small boat across the turbulent waters of the North Sea. Shortly after this, what had become a refugee route for escaping Norwegians became known as the Shetland Bus route, using the same captains and the same boats, but with their main cargo now a mixture of agents and equipment from the SOE being taken into Norway.

Initially on his arrival in the UK he went to London, where he worked as a journalist for the Norwegian government in exile. He carried out this role for eight months before he decided on a change in direction and began studying at military college, from which he graduated in 1943, before he began serving on a Norwegian motor torpedo boat unit. He had still failed to find anything which really excited him, until he enlisted with Kompani Linge and undertook his training in different locations throughout Scotland.

His moment came on New Year's Eve 1944, when, with training over, he was parachuted into Norway over Hadelandsasen, as part of the 'Foscot Plan', to work as an agent for the SOE. The purpose of his mission was to help secure important electrical and telecommunication locations from destruction by the Germans in the ever-increasing likelihood that Germany would lose the war. The Allies believed that in a worst case scenario, retreating German forces would adopt a 'scorched earth' policy. To help Welle-Stand achieve his aims, he established an anti-sabotage training school at Svartasseter.

Erik Welle-Strand, Erling's brother, worked for the Norwegian resistance movement during the war. He had undergone his obligatory military service in 1935 before he began studying at the Norwegian Institute of Technology the following year.

At the beginning of 1940, when he was still a reservist, Eric Welle-Strande was called up and sent to help man an anti-aircraft battery at Bergen. With the invasion by German forces on 9 April 1940, he and his colleagues at the battery became involved in the fighting. When they had all but lost the fight, Norwegian troops began a retreat towards the mountains of Hardanger, whilst still fighting a rear-guard action against the German troops who were chasing them. Welle-Strand split with his comrades and made his way to Tromsø, where he boarded a Royal Navy ship, which took him across the North Sea to the Shetlands.

In September 1940, Britain's Secret Intelligence Service set up a radio communication system which consisted of two stations. One of was located in Oslo and was known by the codeword of Skylark A, with the other being in Trondheim and known as Skylark B. The man in charge of the latter of the two was Erik Welle-Strand. Somewhat fortunately for him, he was instructed in May 1941 to return to London, which he did with the assistance of the Shetland Bus. Why he was recalled exactly is not clear. In his absence, Skylark B still operated but under the leadership of Egil Reksten. In September 1941, the Gestapo finally managed to locate Skylark B's location, which resulted in the arrest of eleven members of the team, seven of whom did not survive the war.

Before the war's end, Welle-Strand returned to Norway via the Shetland Bus to take part in a number of raids along its western coastline. For his wartime efforts he was awarded the St Olav's Medal with Oak Branch, the Haakon VII 70th Anniversary Medal, and the Defence Medal 1940–1945.

Knut Wigert changed his surname from Hansen in 1935. Before the war he was an actor, and in an astonishing twist of fate, whilst working at the National Theatre in Oslo he earned a part as a pilot in a Karl Capek's adaption of an anti-Nazi play, '*The Mother*', the dress rehearsal of which was due to take place on 8 April 1940. In the circumstances and with the German invasion of Norway beginning the very next day, the dress rehearsal never took place, nor did it take place throughout the following five years of German occupation.

During the early days of Nazi rule, Wigert was approached by fellow actor, Martin Linge, to join him as a member of Kompani Linge which he did.

Richard 'Dick' Zeiner-Henriksen was Russian by birth, but moved to Norway early in his life. During the course of the Second World War he was a member of Kompani Linge, which saw him work with Max Manus and the Oslo Gang group of saboteurs.

In May 1944, he was involved in the raid on the Arbeidstjenesten's (Labour Service) offices, but this was called off as there were innocent members of the public present as well. But the group did carry out an attack at another address of the same organisation later that day. Eight men (including Zeiner-Henriksen) carried out the raid, four of whom were from the local Milorg resistance group, during which time they managed to burn hundreds of documents belonging to the Arbeidstjenesten. Three of those who were outside the premises acting as guards, Lars Eriksen, Jon Hartland, and Per Stranger-Thorsen, were captured by German soldiers and executed, the other four escaped, but only Zeiner-Henriksen, Manus and Stryen survived the war. It later transpired that a German collaborator, Hans Eng, had been at the same property earlier the same day.

Zeiner-Henriksen's brother, Erik, who had been a member of the Norwegian resistance movement, had been captured by the Gestapo in May 1944 and was murdered in Dachau concentration camp in February 1945.

The men listed below were also members of the Oslogjengen or the Oslo Gang, two of whom, Gram and Tallaksen, were shot dead by German forces in November 1944.

Gregers Gram
Edvard Tallaksen
Roy Neilsen
Birger Rasmussen
Andreas Aubert
William Houlder
Per Morland
Henrik Hop
Arthur Pevik
Viggo Axelssen

CHAPTER SIX

Allied Military Operations in Norway

Several Allied military operations took place throughout Norway during the course of the Second World War. Those that are known are shown in chronological order.

Operation Wilfred: April 1940

As part of Operation Wilfred, it was agreed that Norwegian territorial waters would be mined by the Royal Navy. The mining of Norwegian waters was originally due to take place on 5 April 1940, but there was an untimely, and what turned out to be a rather unfortunate, delay, with a new date set for 8 April. What was unknown to the British at the time was that on 1 April 1940, Adolf Hitler had ordered the German invasion and occupation of Norway, which then began in earnest on 9 April.

As the British began laying their mines in Norwegian waters on 8 April, it was clear that both sides were unaware of each other's intentions as far as Norway was concerned. The irony was that one of the reasons behind Operation Wilfred was the hope that it would provoke a German response in relation to Norway. It would appear that Germany beat her to it.

The intended follow up operation to Wilfred was known as Plan R 4; a contingency plan that was also due to begin in April

1940 and was only to be launched if Germany invaded Norway. The plan was to land troops and occupy the Norwegian towns of Narvik, Bergen, Stavanger and Trondheim. This caused much debate amongst British politicians because they knew that the implementation of either plan would mean the violation of a neutral country's sovereignty.

Operation Alphabet: 4-8 June 1940

British, French and Polish forces withdrew from the harbour at Narvik on 8 June 1940 as part of Operation Alphabet, which had been authorised on 24 May, two days before the Dunkirk evacuations had begun. During the withdrawal, the British aircraft carrier HMS *Glorious* was attacked and sunk by German battleships *Scharnhorst* and *Gneisenau* in the North Sea, with the loss of 1,200 lives. This was just four days after the last British troops had been successfully evacuated from the beaches of Dunkirk, and less than a month after Winston Churchill had become the British prime minister.

The evacuation saw the end of the Allied campaign in Norway during the Second World War, and had been prompted by Germany's invasion of Belgium, France, Holland and Luxembourg during the spring of 1940, which in effect reduced the importance of Germany's iron ore provision, and of Scandinavia as a whole.

Operation Anklet: 26 December 1941

Operation Anklet was an attack on the Lofoten Islands by 300 men from No. 12 Commando and the Kompani Linge. Those going ashore were ably supported by twenty-two naval vessels from Britain, Norway and Poland, but with no air support provided by the Royal Air Force, a decision that was noted and never repeated. The purpose of the operation was nothing more sinister than a diversionary Allied raid for Operation Archery that was taking place the following day in Vågsøy.

The 300-man raiding party was put ashore on the western side of the island of Moskenesoya, at the southern end of the Lofoten archipelago, at 6 am on 26 December 1941. Of those who took part in the raid, 223 were from No. 12 Commando, and the other 77 were from Kompani Linge. It was hoped that the German defenders would be focusing their attention on Christmas rather than the remote possibility that they might be about to have to deal with an enemy raid. The commandos and the men of Kompani Linge faced no opposition on landing, and remained for two days, occupying two villages, Moskenes and Reine, as well as capturing a German garrison and a number of Norwegian collaborators who they discovered at the Glapen radio station.

Admiral Hamilton, having decided that the raiding party had done its job, called a halt to the raid late on 27 December 1941, and withdrew his men. In part this decision was hastened by an attack from a German seaplane.

Before they departed, the raiders destroyed two radio transmitters. Several German boats were either destroyed or taken, and a number of German soldiers and Norwegian collaborators were captured and taken prisoner. The raiding party did not lose a single man.

A Royal Navy vessel had attacked and sunk a German patrol vessel, but before sending her to the bottom of the sea, had managed to recover a fully working Enigma coding machine, together with its wheels and settings. More than 200 Norwegian civilians also returned with the raiding party, having volunteered to serve in the Free Norwegian Forces, who were stationed in the UK.

Operation Archery: 27 December 1941

On 27 December 1941, Operation Archery took place at Vågsøy in Norway. This saw a force of 570 British commandos from Nos 2, 3, and 4, commando (along with six members of the Kompani Linge and a specialist demolition team from 101 Troop of No. 6 commando). These units were landed by the troop carriers HMS *Prince Charles* and *Prince Leopold.*

The raid was intended to make the Germans not only maintain their numbers in Norway, but to increase them, hopefully through reducing the numbers of men they had deployed on the Eastern Front, which would of course be a great advantage to Britain's Soviet allies.

The operation was a success for the Allies. The raid saw the combined force of British and Norwegian personnel destroy 10 German ships, kill 120 of their men and capture a further 98, whom they took back to England with them. They also acquired a complete copy of the German naval code, which proved to be extremely useful to the British and her allies.

In support of the units that went ashore was a Royal naval artillery bombardment, involving the light cruiser HMS *Kenya*, and the destroyers HMS *Onslow, Oribi, Offa* and *Chiddingfold*, along with air support provided by RAF bombers and fighter bomber aircraft.

The main purpose of the operation was the destruction of a fish oil production plant, a product which was used by the Germans in the production of high explosives to assist in their war effort. To achieve their objective, the commando force of nearly 600 men was divided into five raiding parties. Each had their own target which included securing an area north of the town of Maloy, and engaging any enemy that they came into contact with. They were also tasked with securing the town of Maloy and attacking and eliminating German forces stationed on Maloy Island. Just west of Maloy was a German stronghold at Holvik, which had to be taken. To make sure all of the above went ahead as smoothly as possible, a reserve was kept in readiness off shore on one of the troop ships.

The British authorities also hoped that their daring raid would cause Hitler to increase the number of troops he had stationed in Norway, and by doing so take them away from their duties in other theatres of war.

The day had begun with an early morning naval bombardment of land-based objectives, and the bombardment proved very effective, except in Maloy, where British ground forces came up against much stronger resistance than they had anticipated. What they did not realise was that a unit of battle-hardened German *Gebirgsjäger*, or Mountain Rangers, who had been fighting on the Eastern Front, were in the Maloy area on leave and were able to put up stout defensive action.

The British commandos tasked with taking Maloy quickly found themselves engaged in a house to house scrap, where every building was fiercely fought for. It got to the point where the British commander John Durnford-Slater had to call upon the floating reserve as well as others from Vågsøy Island. Some local citizens even placed themselves in danger by helping the British commandos during the fighting, which meant that they also ran the risk of reprisals by the Germans afterwards. They not only helped by recovering British wounded for treatment, but also helped carry forward much-needed ammunition and grenades. The actions of these individuals were extremely brave.

By early afternoon the task was complete and the British commandos began their withdrawal. The operation had been a success. They had managed to destroy the local telephone exchange, a number of German military installations, four factories, the all-important fish-oil stores, along with ammunition and fuel dumps.

None of the Royal Navy ships was lost, although one of them was struck by a shell fired by a German coastal artillery gun, which killed four naval personnel and wounded a further four.

Captain Martin Linge, a Norwegian and the commander of the Norwegian Armed forces in exile, was one of the casualties: killed during the raid whilst attacking the local German headquarters. The British commandos sustained a number of casualties, which included more than fifty wounded, and, according to the records of the Commonwealth War Graves Commission, six who were killed.

- Lance Sergeant 6010289 William Culling, 32, was a married man who served with the Essex Regiment and No. 3 Commando.

German dead from the *Altmark* incident, February 1940.

German snipers during the invasion of Norway, April 1940.

Above left: Gathering of the Hirden – Norwegian Nazi Paramilitary – at Halden, Norway.

Above right: Kompani Linge Memorial, Glenmore Forest Park, Scotland.

Above left: Lunna House, the original base for the Shetland Bus.

Above right: Max Manus, resistance fighter.

Defeated Norwegian
soldiers at Narvik,
June 1940.

Operation Archery,
27 December 1941.
A raid by British and
Norwegian forces on
Maloy in South Vagsoy.

Above left: Leif Larsen plaque.

Above right: Vidkun Quisling, Heinrich Himmler, Josef Terboven and Nikolaus von Falkenhorst in Norway.

Scalloway Harbour, Shetland.

Crew photograph, 1943.

Above left: Statspolitet, Norway, 1942.

Above right: Erik Gjems-Onstad MBE, Kompani Linge, 1945.

German Troops marching through Bergen, Norway, 1940.

Leif Larsen, 1944.

Above left: Operation Gunnerside team, 1943.

Above right: Little Norway Training Camp, Toronto, Canada, 1940.

Crew of the *Vigra*, 1943.

Norwegian troops arriving at Greenock, Scotland, 1940.

Above left: Leif Larsen statue, Bergen, Norway.

Above right: Memorial at Scalloway, Shetland.

Above left: Haakon VII 70th Anniversary Medal.

Above right: War Medal 1940-1945.

Above left: German surrender of Akershus Fortress to Terje Rollem, 11 May 1945.

Above right: The War Cross (with Sword).

Above left: St Olav's Medal with Oak Branch.

Above right: Captain Harald Sandvik with King Haakon VII and Crown Prince Olav at Glenmore Lodge, Scotland, 1943.

Above: Jens-Anton Poulsson DSO shakes hands with King Haakon VII in 1948.

Left: Memorial in Oslo to members of the Shetland Bus and of the Kompani Linge.

- Lance Sergeant 6344312 Edward James Geear, served with the Queen's Own Royal West Kent Regiment and No. 3 Commando.
- Private 5628235 Peter Hugh Joseph Keast, 25, served with the Devonshire Regiment and No. 3 Commando.
- Private 2879691 James Gardner Murray, 23, served with the 1st Battalion, Gordon Highlanders and No. 3 Commando.
- Lance Corporal 5668915 John Skelton, 31, was a married man who served with the Royal Sussex Regiment and No. 3 Commando.
- Lance Sergeant 3309768 Harold Thomas Andrew Povey, 29, was a married man who served with the Black Watch (Royal Highlanders) and No. 3 Commando.

All six of these men were buried at the Stavne Cemetery in Trondheim, Norway.

The RAF had eight of its aircraft shot down during the course of the raid, which resulted in ten British, one Australian and one New Zealander being killed. Apart from one (Robert Wilson Fisher of the Royal Australian Air Force), all were members of the RAF Volunteer Reserve.

- Sergeant 916359 Clifford Frederick Myhill, served as an observer with No. 235 Squadron.
- Pilot Officer 60530 William Halstead Hughes, 28, was a married man from Harrogate, Yorkshire served with No. 235 Squadron.
- Pilot Officer 62669 Donald Addie Halsall, 21, from Southport, served with No. 254 Squadron.
- Sergeant 941669 Norman Kaby, 22, from Cuddington, Cheshire, served as a pilot with No. 110 Squadron.
- Sergeant 778284 Leonard Frank Redfern served with No. 50 Squadron.

The above five men were buried at the Stavne Cemetery in Trondheim.

- Sergeant 957191 William Frederick George Fletcher, 22, from Letchworth, Hertfordshire and served as a wireless operator and air gunner with No. 114 Squadron.
- Sergeant 1257373 John Edward Kitley served as a wireless operator and an air gunner with No. 114 Squadron.
- Sergeant 997361 John James Burchall Ward served as an observer with No. 114 Squadron.
- Sergeant 1001675 James Williamson served with No. 114 Squadron as an observer.
- Pilot Sergeant 1181613 Kenneth Aubrey Davis 20, from Bromley, Kent, and served with No. 114 Squadron.
- Flight Sergeant 402651 Robert Wilson Fisher, 22, from Nyngan, New South Wales, Australia, and a member of the Royal Australian Air Force, who served with No. 114 Squadron.

The above six men were buried at the Mollendal Church Cemetery in Bergen.

- Flight Lieutenant 403118 Richard Trevor Blewett, 24, from Napier, New Zealand, served as a pilot with No. 110 Squadron. He is buried at the Sola Churchyard, Norway.

Operation Title: 26–31 October 1942

Operation Title saw the fishing boat *Arthur,* operated by Larsen and two colleagues, leave Shetland on 26 October 1942, en route to Norway, with a plan to sink the German battleship *Tirpitz*, which was at anchor in the Trondheim Fjord, an inlet in the Norwegian Sea. Also on board were seven British frogmen and two 'chariots', or miniature submarines. Two days later, on 28 October, the *Arthur* reached the Norwegian coast near the island of Edoya, where it waited for a further two days before unloading the chariots and towing them to their intended target. On 31 October a bad storm broke and the chariots were lost, which resulted in the operation being called off. The next day the decision was made to scuttle the *Arthur* at the village of Breidvik. The three crew members and the seven British frogmen began making their way towards Sweden. Nine of the men escaped, with a tenth, British Agent A. E. Evans, being captured by the Germans and subsequently shot as a spy.

Despite the failure of the operation, Larsen was awarded a Conspicuous Gallantry Medal, making him the first non-British individual to be so decorated. At the time the medal was awarded for gallantry in action for petty officers and seamen of the Royal Navy, and Warrant Officers and other ranks in the Royal Marines. The medal ranked immediately below that of the Victoria Cross in its level of seniority.

Operation Grouse: October 1942 and Operation Freshman: November 1942

In March 1942, the SOE recruited Einar Skinnarland, a Norwegian engineer who worked at the Møsvatn dam. Skinnarland had sailed to Britain and was parachuted back to Telemark after ten days of intensive training. He had several contacts who worked at Vemork hydroelectric power plant who were able to provide him with information about the number of German troops and other defences protecting the facility. Additionally, the SOE decided to send an advance party of Norwegian agents into Telemark, and began intensively training a four-man team over the summer of 1942. The party, code-named Operation Grouse, was led by Jens-Anton Poulsson and included Knut Haugland, Claus Helberg and Arne Kjelstrup. The Norwegians, who were all locals and had exceptional outdoors skills, underwent further outdoor training in Scotland as well as learning the skills necessary to operate in German-occupied Norway, including sabotage, radio transmitting and 'irregular warfare'.

The Grouse team was ready to be inserted by October 1942 and several flights were attempted but then aborted due to bad weather, before the team were finally parachuted in on 18 October. They landed at Fjarifet on the Hardangervidda, a large area of wilderness, and spent the next fifteen days trekking towards Møsvatn, where they made contact with Skinnarland's brother, Torstein. Once they had established contact with London, the party began making preparations for the arrival of the British commandos. A suitable glider-landing site was chosen 3 miles south-west of Møsvatn dam and the team reconnoitred the area to help Combined Operations decide the best way to attack the plant.

The geography of the area around the village and the plant meant that attacking it and destroying the existing stocks of heavy water would be extremely difficult. Both were situated in a deep valley with thickly forested sides that rose almost vertically from a narrow river bed, and which was overlooked by Gaustatoppen, a mountain approximately 5,400ft high; the plant itself had been built on a broad rock shelf 1,000ft above the river bed.

Einar Skinnarland had watched the German defences throughout the summer months of 1942 and passed the information back to the SOE. Details of reconnaissance carried out by Skinnerland and the Grouse team was also sent to London in the weeks leading up to the operation, and included information that in early October, Generaloberst Nikolaus von Falkenhorst, the commander-in-chief of German forces in Norway, had visited the plant. While there, he warned the men guarding it that he believed the plant was a likely target for British commando raids, but despite his concerns he did not have the resources to increase the number of men.

Although Einar Skinnarland had observed a garrison of some 100 men in the village of Rjukan, 20 at the dam and about 55 near the main plant during the summer, by October the number had been reduced to about a dozen at the plant, the same number at the dam, and approximately 40 in Rjukan. Most of the men were elderly or infirm Austrians under the command of an elderly captain, although well-trained German soldiers periodically visited as well.

The Germans had erected three iron hawsers across the valley to prevent low flying Allied bombing raids, but on the ground most of their defences were positioned to prevent an assault from the ridge above the plant, the direction from which they believed an attack was most likely. Minefields and booby traps were the plant's defences, along with searchlights and machine guns near the entrance. With some 300,000 German troops in Norway at this time, it would not have taken reinforcements much time to get to the plant, which would have made things extremely difficult for the commandos escaping to the Swedish border.

This would be the first British airborne operation to use gliders; all previous such operations had been carried out by parachuting men on or near to the intended target. It was decided that gliders would be used for the operation due to the heavy loads that the men would require, along with the possibility that they could be too widely dispersed if they were dropped by parachute. Despite this, the troops were still trained for a possible parachute insertion if it was discovered that the landing zone for the gliders was unsuitable. Because of the complicated and technical nature of the operation, it was believed that a minimum of twelve to sixteen men would be required, and that they would all have to be skilled engineers. The important nature of the operation also led to the force being doubled in order to duplicate it, to ensure that even if half of the force were killed, the survivors would have the necessary skills to complete the operation. Those selected for the operation were volunteers chosen from the sappers of the 9th Field Company Royal Engineers and the 261st Field Park Company, Royal Engineers, who were attached to the 1st Airborne Division.

The SOE agents selected a landing zone for the sappers, which was approximately 3 miles from the Norsk Hydro plant and could not be seen by German patrols. Once they had successfully landed, the sappers would be taken to the plant by the SOE agents, demolish the plant and its stocks of heavy water, and then make their escape by crossing the Norwegian border into neighbouring Sweden.

The first glider carrying one group of commandos took off from RAF Skitten in Scotland at just before 6 pm on 17 November 1942, with the second group following shortly after. The first group flew through poor weather conditions and reached Norway, but, due to onboard technical problems, were unable to locate their intended landing zone. This left the crew of the only aircraft with map-reading available to locate their landing zone, but the poor weather made this almost impossible.

A second attempt to find the correct landing area resulted in the aircraft and glider crashing due to ice at Fyljesdal, overlooking Lysefjord. Of the seventeen men on board, eight were killed outright, four were severely injured and five unhurt. A local farmer, Thorvald Fylgjedalen, discovered some of the injured soldiers from the glider. He and his neighbour Jonas Haaheller decided to help them and the Norwegians sheltered and gave medical attention to the injured soldiers, but did not allow any of them to leave. The Norwegians burned all maps and documents they found from the crashed glider before the Germans arrived the following afternoon and took the British soldiers prisoner. Despite some of them being injured, they were all forced to walk under their own power and ride in the unsheltered boats in the cold.

The aircraft towing the second glider crashed into a mountain, just after releasing its cargo, killing all of those on board. The glider then also crashed near Helleland. Seven of the men were killed in the crash, and the rest were injured to varying degrees. The survivors were unwilling to leave the seriously wounded and two of them went to look for help and in Helleland, some 2 miles away, they made contact with one of the local residents, Trond Hovland. Hovland agreed to help them find a doctor for their injured comrades, but informed them that as the nearest doctor lived nearly 10 miles away, in the town of Egersund, he would have to contact him by telephone. As all calls were listened to by the Germans, the British soldiers decided that it would be better to contact the Germans, expecting that they would be taken as prisoners of war. A party from the Norwegian Labour Service arrived at the crash site shortly afterwards and helped tend to the injured soldiers. German soldiers arrived about twenty minutes later and the British surrendered without a struggle. The prisoners were taken to the German camp at Slettebo near Egersund.

Many of the details about the fate of the men from the two gliders were only discovered after the war had ended. None of the soldiers or aircrew who survived the crashes remained alive for very long. Of the soldiers from the first glider, three of the four injured men were tortured by the Gestapo and later killed by a doctor who injected air into their bloodstreams. The fourth injured man was shot in the back of the head the following day. All four bodies were dumped at sea. The five uninjured men were held at the Grini detention camp until 18 January 1943, when they were then taken to nearby woods, blindfolded and executed by the Gestapo. The German Wehrmacht and the Gestapo argued over the fate of the prisoners from the second glider. The Wehrmacht believed they should be treated in accordance with the Geneva Convention, but in the end the survivors were interrogated and executed within a few hours of their capture, at the German barracks at Bekkebo. They were taken into nearby woods and shot one by one, each being forced to listen to the man before him being executed. Their bodies were stripped and thrown into an unmarked grave. All the executions were conducted in accordance with the Commando Order issued by Hitler in October 1942, which stated that all Commando troops were to be killed immediately upon capture.

Operation Freshman was the codename given to a British airborne operation carried out during November 1942. It was the first British airborne operation to use Airspeed Horsa gliders, with its target being the Vemork Norsk Hydro chemical plant in Telemark, Norway, which produced heavy water for Nazi Germany. The operation was directly linked with Operation Grouse.

The following is a list of the Royal Engineers recorded on the Commonwealth War Graves website as having been killed in Norway on the night of 19 and 20 November 1942. All were buried in Eiganes Churchyard in Stavanger, Norway.

- Sapper 1922713 Herbert J. Legate, served with No. 9 Airborne Field Company.
- Sapper 2010697 James May Stephen, served with No. 261 Airborne Field Park Company.
- Lieutenant Alex Charles Allen, 24, also served with No. 261 Airborne Field Park Company.
- Sapper 1869293 Ernest William Bailey, 31, served with No. 9 Airborne Field Company.
- Driver 2016305 John Thomas Vernon Belfield, 26, was another who served with the No. 261 Airborne Field Park Company.
- Sapper 2074196 Howell Bevan, 22, served with No. 9 Airborne Field Company.
- Lance Corporal 1884418 Frederick William Bray, 29, served with No. 261 Airborne Field Park Company. He was a married man from Edenbridge, Kent.
- Lance Corporal 1923037 Alexander Campbell, 24, was another member of No. 261 Airborne Field Park Company.
- Sapper 2115238 Thomas William Faulkner, 22, was a member of No.9 Airborne Field Company.
- Sapper 1186725 Charles Henry Grundy, 22, served with No. 9 Airborne Field Company.
- Lance Sergeant 4385760 Frederick Healey, 29, served with No. 9 Airborne Field Company.
- Sapper 2110332 John Glen Vernon Hunter, 22, served with No. 9 Airborne Field Company.
- Sapper 2114930 William Jacques, 30, was a married man from Arnold in Nottinghamshire, who served with No. 261 Airborne Field Park Company.

- Lance Sergeant 1871585 George Knowles, 28, was a married man from Bromley in Kent, who served with No. 9 Airborne Field Company.
- Sapper 2110268 Robert Norman, 22, served with No. 9 Airborne Field Company.
- Driver 2000197 Ernest Pendlebury, 25, was a married man from Batley in Yorkshire, who served with No. 261 Airborne Field Company.
- Driver 1884423 George Simkins, 30, was a married man form Romford, Essex, who served with No. 261 Airborne Field Park Company.
- Sapper 2068169 Leslie Smallman was a member of No. 261 Airborne Field Park Company.
- Corporal 2076750 John George Llewellyn Thomas, 23, served with No. 261 Airborne Field Park Company.
- Sapper 1948916 Gerald Stanley Williams, who 18, from Doncaster in Yorkshire, served with No. 9 Airborne Field Company.

The two glider pilots from the Army Air Corps Regiment who were flying Airspeed Horsa gliders, towed by Halifax bomber aircraft from No.38 Group, Royal Air Force, flying out of RAF Skitten, near Wick in Scotland, were:

- Staff Sergeant 320272 Malcolm Frederick Strathdee, served with the 1st Glider Pilot Regiment, Army Air Corps.
- Sergeant 3250420 Peter Doig, 25, served with the 1st Glider Pilot Regiment, Army Air Corps.

The Commonwealth War Graves website does not determine which of the above individuals died when the gliders crashed, or were subsequently executed by the Gestapo.

Interestingly enough, the same website does not show any members of the Royal Air Force who were killed on the same day in Norway, although they show two members of the Australian Air Force, no squadron shown, who died or were killed in Norway on 20 November 1942, and were also buried in the Eiganes Churchyard.

A 20-year-old, Lieutenant 210866 David Alexander Methven of No. 9 Airborne Field Company, Royal Engineers, is also shown as having died or been killed on 20 November 1942, and is buried in the same churchyard. He was a holder of the George Medal, which he had been awarded for an act of bravery on 5 April 1942, when he entered a minefield which had been laid on a beach in the north-east of England. When he arrived at the scene he soon discovered that two men were already dead and a third person, lying some 15 yards into the minefield, was injured. Despite the fact that there were no available plans to show the configuration of the mines, he bravely made his way into the minefield, an area of undulating and drifting sand, to retrieve the injured person.

He had carried out a similar act on Christmas Day 1941, when he entered another minefield and retrieved the body of a dead boy who had wandered into the area.

Operation Musketoon: 11–21 September 1942

Sverre Granlund was 22 years old when, as a soldier in the Norwegian army, he took part in the Battle of Narvik between April and June 1940. After defeat at the hands of the Germans, he remained in Norway until the following year when he eventually escaped to Sweden, before making his way to the UK where he joined the SOE and became a member of Kompani Linge.

He was returned to Norway on a boat of the Shetland Bus on 27 May 1941, as part of a raiding party involved in an attack on a fish factory in Bodo.

The following year he took part in Operation Musketoon, which was a commando raid on the Glomfjord power plant. The operation involved a twelve-man team, ten of whom were British, whilst Granlund and Corporal **Erling Djupdraet** were the two

Norwegian members. After the target of the raid had been achieved and the local dam was breached, the team began the not-so-easy task of trying to escape. There was no boat, submarine or aircraft ready and waiting to pick them up, so it was up to every man to try get back to England the best way he could.

Djupdraet was wounded the following day when he became involved in an unrelated disagreement with some German soldiers who were unaware that he was one of those who had been involved in the sabotage at the Glomfjord power plant. In the ensuing scuffle, one of the German soldiers stabbed Djupdraet with his rifle bayonet. He subsequently died of his wounds in hospital at Bodo on 24 September 1942.

By the end of the war, only two of the men who took part in the raid, Lance Sergeant Richard O'Brien and Private John Fairclough, had survived.

To escape via Sweden, Granlund undertook a walk of some 160 miles which took him seven days, meaning that he walked on average just under 23 miles a day, a feat he achieved with practically no food or water.

Granlund died on 10 February 1943 when the Norwegian submarine *Uredd,* on which he was travelling as part of Operation Seagull, struck a German mine and sank south-west of Fugloyvaer, although the Norwegian Royal Navy only officially reported the loss on 20 February 1943. There were no survivors.

Operation Carhampton: 31 December 1942–1 March 1943

This was a British and Norwegian special forces undertaking by the newly formed Special Operations Executive. The plan was to intercept and capture shipping off the west coast of German-occupied Norway during January and February 1943. The origins of the undertaking lay with Odd Kjell Starheim, a Norwegian resistance fighter and SOE agent. More about the operation and Starheim can be found in the next chapter.

Operation Seagull: 10 February 1943

Operation Seagull was a British-led operation to destroy several industrial targets in German-occupied Norway, including a smelter at Arendal. The Norwegian submarine, HNoMS *Uredd* was taking the men to Bodo, when she hit a mine laid by the German minelayer, *Cobra* and sank. The crew of thirty-four and the six-man Special Operations Executive team, who were on board, were all killed. The six men of SOE, all Norwegians, were:

- Lieutenant Per Getz
- Sub Lieutenant Tobias Skog
- Sergeant Thorlief Daniel Grong
- Corporal Sverre Granlund
- Private Eivind Dahl Erikson
- Private Hans Rohde Hansen

Their names are all recorded on a war memorial in Dundee.

Operation Gunnerside: February 1943

The operation took place over 27/28 February 1943; its aim was to blow up heavy-water facilities in Norway in order to sabotage the efforts of the German nuclear energy project.

On 16 February 1943, six Norwegian commandos were dropped in to Norway by parachute from a Halifax bomber of No. 138 Squadron. Once safely on the ground they met up with members of Operation Grouse, who were still operational and were now referred to as Operationan Swallow.

On the night of 27/28 February, members of the team entered the Vemork Plant via a cable tunnel, placed timed explosives on the heavy-water electrolysis chambers, which left them sufficient time to escape. The raid was a total success, halting production at the plant for several months. The entire stock of heavy water that had been produced at the plant up to that time was destroyed, along with critical equipment needed for the plant's electrolysis chambers.

Some 3,000 German soldiers were sent to the area to search for the saboteurs, all of whom successfully escaped. Four of the team remained in the area to carry out further resistance work. Two of them made their way to Oslo to team up with members of the Norwegian resistance movement, and the remaining five skied a distance of some 250 miles to reach the safety of Sweden.

Operation Martin: 29 March 1943

In early 1943, Jan Sigurd Baalsrud and three fellow commandos made their way across the North Sea to Norway on board a vessel of the Shetland Bus, which had a crew of eight. The reason for their journey was a mission to destroy the control tower at the German-controlled airfield at Bardufoss in northern Norway, and to recruit individuals from the local population to join the Norwegian resistance movement. The mission, which had been given the code name Operation Martin, was compromised early on. On landing in Norway, Baalsrud and his comrades attempted to make contact with a trusted member of the Norwegian resistance, but instead made contact with a shopkeeper who had the same name. This was where the mission started to go wrong, because the shopkeeper got into a bit of a panic believing he was 'set up' by the Germans to test his 'loyalty'. He did no more than report the incident to the local police, who, fearing the same as the shopkeeper, decided to pass the same information on to the German authorities.

The following morning, 29 March 1943, a boat of the Shetland Bus, the *Brattholm,* which had more than 100kg of high explosive on board for use by Baalsrud and his colleagues to blow up the airfield's control tower, was spotted and attacked by a German naval vessel. Not wanting to be captured or have their cargo discovered, the crew placed a timer on the explosives, the detonation of which sank their vessel, whilst they attempted to escape in a small boat. The German vessel, which was soon upon them, quickly opened fire, sinking their boat in the process. All eight of the crew were killed. Baalsrud and his colleagues decided to take their chances in the cold icy waters of the North Sea and swam ashore, with Baalsrud being the only one of them to evade capture. He hid in a gully until he gathered his thoughts. Minus one of his boots, wet through and as cold as it was possible to be without being unconscious, he initially managed to evade capture. Before long he was discovered by a Gestapo officer, but still having his wits about him, Baalsrud drew his pistol and shot the German dead.

Somewhat remarkably in the severe wintery conditions, he managed to stay at large for more than two months, despite suffering from frostbite and snow blindness, the latter being a painful eye condition caused by exposure of insufficiently protected eyes to the ultraviolet rays from either natural or artificial light.

His worsening condition forced him to find help. He kept his fingers crossed, hoping that on this occasion he was approaching the right people, and not those that would likely report him to the German authorities.

To emphasise just how bad a physical condition he was in, Baalsrud was forced to amputate one of his big toes, and part of the toe next to it, with nothing more sophisticated than a pocket knife, as he feared that he might have gangrene and did not want it to spread.

Whilst being looked after by helpful townsfolk from the town of Manndalen in Kafjord, he was moved up into the surrounding hills and mountains to escape the attention of an ever-increasing number of German patrols. It was for his safety as well as theirs. The penalty for helping and hiding an enemy agent would have been death. But although Baalsrud had not been left in the comfort of a structure such as a log cabin with a blazing fire for company, some thought had been given to his wellbeing. He had been left near to a big rock, which had then been surrounded by a natural-looking wall of snow, providing a void he could hide behind. Left with food and supplies and trying to stay as warm as possible, he remained there for twenty-seven days. When the townsfolk came to collect him, they discovered that he had cut off nine more of his toes to help prevent the spread of gangrene. Once again, he had carried out the 'surgery' with his trusty pocket knife.

Baalsrud was carried by stretcher to the nearby border with Finland, where he was looked after by some native Fins who took him across country, where arrangements had been made for him to be collected by a seaplane operating on behalf of the Red Cross and flown to Boden in the southern part of Sweden. He spent several months in hospital recovering from his injuries and infection, before being flown back to Britain.

Rather than put his now toeless feet up and take a more sedate desk job, in the knowledge that he had done his bit, he returned to Shetland to help train fellow Norwegians who wanted to return to their country to fight against the tyranny of their German occupiers. But was still not content. He pushed himself to learn how to walk properly once again; no easy achievement. His next challenge was to convince the authorities, which included his bosses at the SOE, to let him return to Norway as an agent. Remarkably, when Germany surrendered and Norway once again became a free nation, Baalsrud was still there working on active service as an agent.

With the war finally over, and his country liberated from German occupation, he was once again able to return to his family in Oslo, whom he had not seen for five years.

Both Britain and his native Norway were grateful to Baalsrud for his wartime efforts and showed their gratitude in the form of awards. Britain made him an honorary Member of the Order of the British Empire, the best that they could do for a non-British subject. As for Norway, they awarded him the St Olav's Medal with Oak Branch, for

> Outstanding services rendered in connection with the spreading of information about Norway abroad and for strengthening the bonds between expatriate Norwegians and their home country.

Operation Mardonius: 27 April 1943

Operation Mardonius resulted in the blowing up of two German naval vessels, the *Ortelsburg* and the *Tugela,* in Oslo harbour. Once again this was a well-planned operation, the method of which was changed on more than one occasion and required approval from military figures in London. The plan eventually agreed upon was one drawn up by Max Manus and Gregers Gram, but before it went ahead, proof was needed to show that there was a realistic chance of the operation being successful; this was achieved through a number of experiments and a significant amount of training in the UK.

Once everything was ready, Manus and Gram were parachuted back into Norway, landing at Ostmarka near Oslo on 12 March 1943, with a number of weapons, ancillary equipment and provisions. Having arrived, there was no immediate rush. Surviving such operations was often achieved in the planning stage. Once they were ready, the operation went ahead on 27 April 1943, and along with **Einar Riis** and **Halvor Haddeland**, two local resistance fighters, Manus and Gram paddled two canoes out to the tiny island of Bleikoya, where they had earlier stored items they would need to carry out their operation. The four men waited patiently and quietly until darkness fell, but because of a lack of cloud cover it was not quite as dark as they hoped it would be. Having considered all the variables, the decision was made that they would go ahead with the operation.

The teams were split so that an SOE operative was with one of the local resistance fighters. Gram and Haddeland rowed their canoe to the *Ortelsburg*, where they placed four time-delayed limpet mines on its hull and the same on the hull of the nearby *Sarpfoss.* In the meantime, Manus and Riis made their way to the *Gronlia*, where they attached similar limpet mines to its hull. They had also intended to do the same with the *Winrich von Kniprode*, but changed their minds due to it being brightly lit whilst night-time work was being carried out on it.

With their operation successfully carried out, the four men rowed their canoes back to dry land, where Manus and Gram escaped to the Swedish capital of Stockholm and later from there to England.

On 28 April 1943, the limpet mines placed on the *Ortelsburg* exploded, sinking the ship within a matter of minutes. Explosions followed on the *Bleikoya* and the *Tugela,* as did one that had been placed on a barge. The limpet mines on the *Sarpfross* failed to detonate.

At Nethy Bridge, Scotland, in June 1943, King Haakon of Norway presented Manus and Gram with the Norwegian War Cross with Sword for the bravery and valour displayed by both men during Operation Mardonius.

Both men returned to Norway on a vessel of the Shetland Bus in October 1943 to take part in further SOE operations. Gram was shot dead during a gunfight with Gestapo officers in Norway in November 1944.

Operation Vestige: 3 September 1943–8 May 1945

Vestige was not just a single operation, but eight operations carried out by members of the Special Operations Executive over a twenty-one month time period, between 3 September 1943 and 8 May 1945. The first three ran simultaneously between 3 September and 16 November 1943: Vestige I, consisted of a three-man team, whilst Vestige II and Vestige III both consisted of two-man teams.

The plan involved attacking German shipping along the west coast of Norway by covertly attaching limpet mines to the sides of the ships. The three-man Norwegian team of Operation Vestige I included Harald Svindseth, Ragnar Ulstein and Nils Fjeld, who after being dropped off by a motor torpedo boat, covered the area between Bergen and Alesund. On the night of 23/24 September, the team placed limpet mines on the side of the German freighter *Hermut,* which was in the Gulenfjord, north of Bergen. When the mines detonated, the ship only avoided sinking because her captain reacted quickly enough to run her ashore. The three-man team managed to escape and were picked up by a motor torpedo boat on 16 November.

Operation Vestige II also commenced on 3 September, when the two-man team of L. Olsen and I. Naess, were dropped off by a motor torpedo boat. Initially their intention was to attack German shipping at anchor in Askvoll harbour, but they had to cancel their plans due to poor weather, which was obviously exaggerated by the fact that they were in a canoe. The two men moved on to Alesund where they joined up with the Operation Antrum team, with whom they remained until they were picked up 17 November.

Operation Vestige III again began on 3 September, the two-man team being S. Synnes and H. Hoel. On 6 October they attacked the German freighter *Jantje Fritzen* in Alesund. Despite all six of the limpet mines attached to the ship's hull having detonated, it managed to stay afloat and was towed to Bergen for repair. Synnes and Hoel were collected along with the Vestige II team on 17 November.

Operation Vestige IV began in March 1944, and consisted of Norwegians K. Idsand, A. Akre and K. Enresen. As far as it is known they were only able to sink one small vessel that they discovered in Flekkefjord harbour. But despite their lack of success, they remained operational for the rest of the war, albeit their orders were changed in the early weeks of 1945, when they were ordered to carry out acts of sabotage against German military camps.

Operation Vestige V, which took place between 31 March and 9 May 1944, concentrated on the waters around the island of Stord at Sagvag. The two-man team of K. Vilnes and P. Orstenvik specifically targeted German vessels that were laden with pyrites, but the men were hampered in their attempts by inclement weather. The two men were collected by a submarine chaser boat on 9 May, having been unsuccessful in their attempts.

Operation Vestige VIII was put in to place on 12 April and consisted of a two-man team, H. Hoel and I. Naess. Hoel had been a member of Operation Vestige III, whilst Naess had been part of Operation Vestige II. The idea was for the two men to attack shipping in the Malm area of northern Trondelag. The operation once again failed due to the poor weather and a lack of darkness due to the long days and short nights at that time of the year, and the two men were recovered on 1 May.

Operation Vestige XII was instigated on 16 March 1944, with the plan of attacking shipping in the Soderfjord with a three-man team of A. Torkildsen, A. Gade-Torp and F. Brandt. Rather than using fixed canoes, they used folding ones which were better at being moved from point to point across land. Once again the operation was unsuccessful and the men had to escape by making their way to Sweden.

Operation Vestige XIV began on 31 March 1944, when the three-man team of R. Larsen, O. Hansen and B. Petersen were dropped by aircraft, in diving suits and with folding canoes, to carry out attacks on shipping in Frederisckstad and Ostfold ports. Whilst en route to carry out an attack they were discovered by German soldiers. A firefight ensued and the three Norwegians managed to escape unscathed to Sweden.

Operation Source: 21 September 1943

The German battleship *Tirpitz*, anchored at Kafjord in the Troms og Finnmark county, was attacked by a number of British midget submarines. Although not sunk, she was damaged badly enough to put her out of action for more than six months.

Operation Company: November 1943

On 12 November 1943, Edvard Tallaksen returned to Norway, this time by parachute, along with **Birger Rasmussen** and **Armand Trønnes**, as part of Operation Company. This saw the men infiltrate the Arendal Smelters' works and blow up five generators, whilst ensuring that none of the facility's civilian workers were injured or killed. The three men then hid for a period of two weeks whilst German forces were looking for them. Once they felt it was safe to make a move, they made their way to Oslo where they joined up with the Milorg resistance group, whose personnel they began training.

Operation Osprey: 10 December 1943

Alf Espedel served with Kompani Linge and took part in Operation Osprey, which parachuted into Rogaland County on 10 December 1943.

Operation Lapwing: 1943

During 1943, a group of men serving with Kompani Linge, and led by Reidar Kvaal, were parachuted in to the mountain region of Haltdalen, where they operated behind enemy lines. For his service during that time, Kvaal was awarded the Military Cross by the British authorities, and St Olav's Medal with Oak Branch by Norway.

Operation Sunshine: October 1944 – May 1945

Operation Sunshine was an anti-demolition operation carried out in German-occupied Norway between October 1944 and May 1945. It was planned by Leif Tronstad at the Norwegian Ministry of Defence in London, in co-operation with British forces, and was part of an effort to protect identified essential Norwegian installations and industry, in particular the large power stations at Notodden, Kongsberg and Nore, from being destroyed in a possible scorched earth action by the retreating Germans towards the end of the Second World War.

Nine men were selected for the operation and were parachuted in under the cover of darkness over Ugleflott in Ovre Telemark on the evening of 5 October 1944. The man in charge of the operation, Major Leif Tronstad, was killed action in March 1945, having taken a local bailiff hostage.

Operation Fieldfare: 7 March 1944 – 8 May 1945

Operation Fieldfare was a British operation carried out by members of the Special Operations Executive between 7 March 1944 and 8 May 1945, involving observations of the railway system which linked Andalsnes and Dombas in German-occupied Norway. They also compiled weapons and explosives dumps near the railway lines, and prepared plans to counter German defensive measures along the same railway link.

There were only three men in the unit: Jochim Rønneberg, Birger Strømsheim and Olav Aarsæther. They parachuted in to Norway on the night of 7/8 March, but lost much of their equipment in a bad landing. The party did receive further supplies, but not for another four months, in July 1944, after which they had to survive on just meagre rations until Norway was liberated. Despite being in Norway for fourteen months, the team only undertook a solitary act of sabotage on the railway line, on 5 January 1945. In March 1945, Rønneberg travelled back to the UK but returned in May to help in the liberation of Alesund.

Operation Cheese: Throughout the Second World War in Norway

Operation Cheese was an intelligence operation carried out in Norway throughout the course of the Second World War, and which saw a radio station being set up at Tomstad's farm at Helle, just outside the town of Flekkefjord in southern Norway. It was Odd Starheim, a resistance fighter and SOE agent, and Gunvald Tomstad, a double agent, who first established wartime radio communications between Norway and the UK.

Operation Jupiter: Never took place

Operation Jupiter never actually took place, but I still believe it is worth a mention. It was the code name for a plan, which originated in 1941, for an invasion of northern Norway and Finland by Allied forces during the Second World War. The operation had a number of operational code names during the planning stages, including Operation Dynamite, Operation Ajax and Operation Marrow. It was the brainchild of, and vigorously promoted by, Winston Churchill, but it was opposed by all the senior British and Allied commanders, who considered it impractical because of insufficient air support and because they felt it was of limited value. The scheme was eventually abandoned in favour of the Normandy landings.

CHAPTER SEVEN

Boats and Men of the
Shetland Bus

There is a memorial on the waterfront at Scalloway to those who
died whilst participating in the work of the Shetland Bus during the
Second World War. It is in the form of a round cairn, made out of
stone taken from both Shetland and Norway. There is a sculpture
on top of the cairn: a depiction of the *Andholmen* riding the crest
of a wave. The vessel was one of those used as a Shetland Bus. The
side of the cairn includes four metal name plaques.

Somewhat amazingly, the memorial was only unveiled on
21 June 2003, some fifty-eight years after the end of the war and the
last sailing of the Shetland Bus. The inscription on the plaque reads:

> The Shetland Bus 1940–1945
> Alt For Norge
> We remember with deep respect and gratitude
> All who contributed to the work of the Shetland Bus
> In Shetland, in Norway and on the stormy seas between.
> They gave their all for Freedom.

The following are stories about the vessels and men who made their
way into German-occupied Norway by means of the Shetland Bus
operation. Some survived, but many did not.

Appendices I & II list the Norwegians who died whilst in service of the Shetland Bus and the vessels that were lost.

Ingvald Johansen and the M/B *Vita* – May 1941

The M/B *Vita* was one of the original Shetland Bus boats, in that it had been doing the Norway-Shetland run before the Shetland Bus came into existence. With only a 40-horse-power engine, it was not the most powerful of vessels to traverse the torrid waters of the North Sea, but it certainly did the job. It first arrived in Shetland on 9 May 1940, whilst the Norwegian armed forces were still doing their best to stave off the invasion of their country, and four of those on board the *Vita* were Norwegian naval officers. With the fighting still having a month to run, it now appears a strange event to have taken place when it did. Surely four military officers could have been better utilised in the defence of their country than skipping the country on a fishing boat? There were also two civilian refugees on board the *Vita* on that same voyage.

It was some seven months before the *Vita* undertook a return journey to Norway, on 22 December 1940, and after that it was 27 March 1941. From the latter of those two dates the *Vita's* skipper was Ingvald Johansen, and his four-man crew was made up of Age Sandvik, H. W. Olsen, Jens Haldorsen and J. Hermansen.

In May 1941, the *Vita* took part in an amazing rescue in the North Sea. The M/B *Signal* was only 60 miles into its journey from Norway to Shetland, when without prior warning her engine stopped and, despite their best efforts, her crew were unable to restart it. She was at the mercy of the sea; just one rogue wave could have enveloped her and taken her and her crew to a watery grave.

The *Vita* managed to get close enough to rescue the twelve refugees who were on board the *Signal*. It is not clear as to what happened to the vessel and her crew, but it is possible that the *Vita* towed the *Signal* and her crew back to Norway, before returning to Shetland with the refugees.

When it came to rules of secrecy, the Shetland Bus operation was no different from other such clandestine groups in being expected to adhere to them without question. But there was always one who would sometimes push the boundaries, sometimes possibly too far, and in doing so endanger their lives as well as the lives of others, whether that was crew or refugees. On one such journey, the skipper of the *Vita*, Ingvald Johansen, on arriving in Norway, posted a letter to his fiancée, which contained the time, date and location of his next arrival in Norway, asking her to meet him and return with him to Shetland. Allowing for the state of mind that the emotions of love can place an individual in, this was an act of utter madness. This letter could have been intercepted by the German authorities, which would have resulted in the arrest and detention of Johansen, his fiancée and his crew – with potentially fatal outcomes for all.

Fortunately, the letter was not intercepted, Johansen's fiancée turned up at the allotted time, date and location, and returned to Shetland, where she and Johansen were subsequently married. The British authorities took no action against him for this chronic breach of security. On this occasion Johansen was one very lucky individual, something which his fiancé and crew would have been extremely happy about.

Between May and September 1941, Johansen and the *Vita* made a number of return journeys between Shetland and the Norwegian coast without a single hitch, other than the odd bit of bad weather. All that changed, however, on 22 September 1941. Having left Shetland the previous day, they arrived at Rekoy in North Trondelag. The intention was to pick up a number of refugees who they would take straight back to Shetland. This was one of those occasions when things did not quite go according to plan. Unfortunately a Norwegian collaborator, who was aware of the collection of the refugees from Rekoy, informed the Germans of what he knew. The obvious speculation about the identity of this individual strongly suggests that he was one of the intended refugees, and for a sum of Nazi money, was more than willing to 'dob in' his fellow Norwegians to the Germans.

This action resulted in the arrest of Johansen and his crew, and their imprisonment for the rest of the war. In the circumstances, it was not too bad an outcome for all concerned, as there would have been some amongst the Germans, especially the Gestapo, who would have wanted them executed on suspicion of espionage.

As for the *Vita,* it was used by the Germans throughout the rest of the war, spending its days sailing up and down the west coast of Norway, trying to catch similar boats from escaping the country with refugees. At the end of the war, the *Vita* reverted to being a fishing vessel.

The *Nordsjøen* – 20 October 1941

The *Nordsjøen* was a minelayer skippered by a man named Gjertsen. It was sunk in heavy weather off of the coast of West Norway on 20 October 1941. Somewhat miraculously in the circumstances, all of the ship's crew survived. They were picked up by fellow Shetland Bus vessel, the M/K *Arthur* and arrived back in Shetland on 31 October.

Nils Nesse and the M/B *Siglaos* – 28 October 1941

One of the crew of the *Siglaos,* 23-year-old Nils Nesse, who was from Bremnes on the island of Bomlo, south of Bergen, was the first crewman of a vessel of the Shetland Bus to be killed during the Second World War.

On 28 October 1941, the *Siglaos* was returning to Shetland from Norway after successfully dropping off an agent, equipment and supplies, when it was attacked by a German aircraft. The pilot fired his machine guns into the very heart of the boat, safe in the knowledge that the crew were unable to defend themselves, which strongly suggests that the pilot had no idea of the work that the *Siglaos* was involved in.

A damaged *Siglaos* made it back to Shetland. Nesse was buried in the churchyard of the parish church at Lunna Kirk. That is where his body remained until 1948, when his coffin was exhumed and taken back to Norway for reburial, but a cross in the churchyard marks the spot where his grave was.

Ingvald Lerøy and the M/K *Blia* – 14 November 1941

The M/K *Blia* left Norway on 14 November 1941, en route to Shetland. Captain of the vessel was 21-year-old Ingvald Lerøy, and along with his six crew members, he had on board thirty-five Norwegian refugees. On the night of the journey, the weather was particularly bad, with a strong possibility of storms forecast.

The *Blia* never made it to Shetland with her crew and thirty-five refugees; she was never seen or heard of again. It is a mark of how determined individuals were to escape from Norway that they would even make the journey in the first place, at night, in storm conditions during the middle of a harsh winter. It also shows how brave the crew of the *Blia* were that they were prepared to go to sea to try and help their fellow Norwegians to escape to freedom. Six of the crew were 25 years old or younger.

In addition to the story about the *Blia,* when she left Norway on 11 November 1941 she had to leave approximately forty more people behind because there was not enough room on the boat. These same forty individuals eventually did safely make it to Scotland on board another fishing vessel from Norway later than month.

The unpredictable weather of the North Sea during the winter months is quite possibly the main reason why so many journeys of the Shetland Bus went ahead without any sight or intervention by a German boat or aircraft, because they simply did not suspect that a regular service between Norway and Shetland would take place across such treacherous waters.

Arne Roald, Sevrin Roald, Olav Røsvik and the M/K *Heland* – 27 February 1942

M/K *Heland* was owned by three men from Vigra in the Møre og Romsdal county, on the west coast of Norway. The men concerned were brothers Sevrin and Arne Roald, along with a friend of theirs, Olav Røsvik. The *Heland* was a relatively new vessel having only been built in 1937, and at some 60ft in length with an 85hp engine, she was certainly a powerful enough vessel. She was a ship from which her owners earned their living, fishing in the waters of the North Sea.

Heland's first journey for the Shetland Bus took place on 14 November 1941, when just one of its three owners, Sevrin Roald, skippered it. This was the same night that the M/K *Blia* was lost during horrendous weather conditions, and on the same route as the M/K *Heland* had taken. Beside the ship's crew there were two passengers on board, both men were members of Kompani Linge, Karl Johan Aarsaeter and Asmund Wisloff, making them the very first agents officially to use the Shetland Bus.

Heland had used the false name of M/K *Per* for the journey. As soon as the boat arrived in Shetland, it quickly offloaded its two agents, refuelled, took on board supplies for other agents who were in Norway, and then disappeared into the eye of the storm to return to her Norway home as quickly and as safely as was possible. There was no waiting for morning because they needed to complete as much of the journey as possible under the cover of darkness, even if it did mean travelling in bad weather, to avoid being spotted by German aircraft.

On 27 February 1942, having left Norway the *Heland* once again made the dangerous journey across the North Sea, and once again Sevrin Roald was her skipper. But this was no ordinary journey. Roald had his wife, Inga, with him, but not for her company or to cook for the crew and others on board, for him this was his chance to escape the Nazi occupation of his country. For them, there was no return journey, no more having to fight their way across the North Sea, never knowing if they would ever see each other again. From then on they became part of the land crew in the Shetland Bus operation, and were based in Scalloway.

There was a big advantage to having them on the land crew, because many men, if not most of them, were on their own when they first arrived in Shetland having escaped their homeland, so having a happy, smiling married couple to greet them was a godsend for many.

On that final journey for Sevrin Roald, besides his wife and crew there were a total of twenty-three Norwegian refugees, including Trygve Stein Rypdal, his wife Sylvi, their 8-year-old son Arild and 3-year-old Trygve. Prior to their departure, Rypdal had been the district leader of the Milorg resistance movement in the Alesund area. Life had become rather dangerous for him; the Germans were closing in on him and so it was time to go.

Others on board the *Heland* included Olaf Hahjem, Johan Hagbart Molnes, Nils Johan Molnes, Sverre Johan Molnes, Harald Peter Ratvik, Arne Ottar Roald, Arnfinn Sevrin Roald, Bjarne Jon Roald, Harald Gunnar Roald, Inga Emilie Roald, Joe Bernt Andersen Roald, Karl Johan Roald, Sverre Normann Roald, Arnfinn Oddmund Roaldsnes, Karl Sigvart Roaldnes, Jakob Peder Rorvik, Bernt Skodje and Jakob Skodje.

It was clear to see from the numbers of his extended family Sevrin Roald had brought with him on the journey, not only was this ever intended to be a one-way trip, but he wanted to make sure that none of his family were left behind for the Germans to then vent their frustration and annoyance on.

Roald's boat the *Heland* did not go to waste, as it was still used as part of the Shetland Bus programme, just without him as skipper. The man to whom that job fell for most of the subsequent trips was August Nerø, but there were others as well. There were one or two occasions when things did not quite go according to plan, but those who skippered her always managed to get her safely back to Shetland. With the arrival of the American submarine chasers in October 1943, *Heland* became surplus to requirements and was officially classified as a reserve vessel; only used for the transfer of supplies or for short journeys in and around Scottish waters, between Shetland and the UK mainland.

The *Heland* survived the war and afterwards returned to Norway to once again become a fishing vessel. In the early 1970s it was donated to the museum in Sunmore in the county of Møre og Romsdal, whose main city is Alesund, where it was preserved as one of the fishing vessels of the Shetland Bus fleet. Because of what it represented, and still represents, for the Norwegian people, its placing at the Sumore Museum is all important for future generations of Norwegians.

Knut Årsæter and the M/B *Frøya* – April 1942

The M/B *Frøya*, a 60-ft long fishing vessel, first arrived in Shetland on 16 March 1942, having like many of her counterparts, left Norway for the safety of the UK. On board was Knut Årsæter, an agent with Kompani Linge, along with four men from the Alesund area: Lauritz Barstad, Mindor Fiksdal, Didrik Naero, and Erling Vestre. The owner of the boat, Karl Giskegjerde, who had agreed to his boat being used by the group, asked that they made it look as if they had stolen it. If the German authorities believed for one second that he had willingly allowed his vessel to be used by the group to travel to the UK, the consequences for him could have been dire. One aspect of the incident which went in his favour, and made it appear to have been a theft, was that it took place right in the middle of the lucrative herring season.

The *Frøya* became part of the Shetland Bus operation, and at the end of April, left Scotland on a mission to Troms in northern Norway. On board were a crew of seven along with two agents. As the *Frøya* approached its destination off the Norwegian coast, it was attacked by a German aircraft, whose bombs did their intended job. Slowly but noticeably, the *Frøya* began to sink. Thankfully for the crew, their 12ft-long lifeboat was not damaged in the attack. But this still resulted in a difficult decision as the *Frøya's* captain decided it would be dangerous for all nine of them to attempt to get in it. The captain and three of the crew quickly put together a makeshift raft from some of the boat's empty oil barrels, threw it into the sea, and climbed on board. This left the remaining five men to get into the lifeboat, but in heavy seas it very quickly began filling with water, leaving the men no option but to continually bail out the boat so that it could stay afloat.

As the weather conditions improved so those on board the lifeboat were able to hoist the sail and steer, as best they could, in the general direction of Scotland. Although they had survived the sinking of the *Frøya,* their problems quickly began. To begin with they lost sight of their four colleagues on the raft, and the realisation that they had neither food nor water soon hit home. All they could do was stay strong for as long as they could and cling on to the hope that they would either soon reach safety or be rescued by a passing ship. As one day became the next, and with only what rainwater they could catch to drink, the lack of food started to become a problem.

After more than a week, they were overwhelmed with joy and relief when they spotted land. Although they did not know it, what they had seen was Muckle Flugga, a small rocky island north of Unst in Shetland; often wrongly described as the northernmost point of the British Isles.

No sooner had they spotted land, albeit some miles away from where they were, they were seen by a passing ship and rescued. Once safely on board they informed the captain of the plight of their comrades who were bobbing around somewhere in the North Sea on nothing more substantial than a raft made of empty oil drums, and in no time at all British ships and aircraft were out searching for them.

Out of the five men who were rescued from the lifeboat, two of them had suffered greatly and were in an extremely bad way, both of them requiring hospital treatment. So determined were the three other men to help find their lost colleagues, that after a good night's sleep and a hearty breakfast, they were up and out on board one of the boats involved in the search.

Per Blystad and the M/B *Olaf* – 17 April 1942

The M/B *Olaf* was a 52-ft fishing vessel with a 60hp engine owned by Ansgar Sønderland and Johan O. Rørvik, which had first arrived in Lerwick on 30 September 1941 with seventeen refugees who had escaped from Norway. Although they were not on board, the boat's two owners had given their permission for it to be used to take their fellow countrymen to freedom. Rather than just rotting away in Lerwick, the boat, which was neither particularly big or powerful, was given to the SOE and become part of the Shetland Bus operation, with its new skipper being Norwegian Per Blystad.

After a bit of a spruce up and a couple of alterations, she was ready for service. Her new crew were: skipper Per Blystad, Olai Hillersøy, Arne Nipen, Leif and Olav Kinn, and during the winter of 1942, the *Olaf* made five return journeys across the North Sea between Shetland and Norway, ferrying agents, refugees, supplies and equipment between the two locations. Its importance to the Shetland Bus operation could be measured in the number of times it was attacked by German aircraft, and survived.

The most notable of these trips was undoubtedly the one which took place on 17 April 1942, when it delivered two agents, Arne Værum and Emil Hvaal from Kompani Linge to Telavåg. Soon after they had been spotted clambering ashore, somebody had informed the German authorities that there were two Norwegian soldiers being hidden by the residents of Telavåg, and so a number of Gestapo officers turned up in the town on 26 April 1942. The information about the exact location of the two agents was accurate, but when the Gestapo went to the particular address to arrest them, a gunfight ensued. In the exchange of shots, two members of the Gestapo were killed along with Arne Værum. Hvaal was taken alive, but a few months later he was executed by firing squad, along with his son.

But that was not the end of the matter. The Germans' revenge was swift and extensive, as well as being extremely brutal. Every boat in the coastal village was either sunk or confiscated. All of their livestock was taken away, and every property in the village was burnt to the ground. All but seventy-two of the villages' adult males were executed. The men who survived, along with the women and children, were either imprisoned or sent to the Sachsenhausen concentration camps, where thirty-one of them were murdered and others perished from disease or illness.

The man responsible for these reprisals was the country's Reichskommissar, Josef Terboven, mentioned previously.

In some respects, *Olaf* could be classed as a very lucky boat, as despite having been attacked by German aircraft on several occasions, she never sank. However, her time as an active vessel of the Shetland Bus came to an abrupt end on 12 May 1942. She was involved in a search of the North Sea looking for a wooden raft that had four men from the stricken vessel, the *Frøya,* on it. Three of her crew who had already been rescued were also part the *Olaf's* crew that day. A German Dournier bomber aircraft spotted the *Olaf* and then attacked her on a number of occasions in quick succession. This resulted in her sustaining a severe amount of damage, and some of her crew were injured and wounded. One of those from the crew of the *Frøya,* Hans Johansen, later died as a result of his injuries.

Although the *Olaf* only just made it back to shore and had its damage repaired, it did not make any subsequent journeys as part of the Shetland Bus operation. At the end of the war the boat was returned to its owners in Norway.

In the meantime, the search for the four crew members of the *Frøya,* who had to make do with the makeshift raft of oil drums continued, but was called off after a few days, with everybody understandably assuming the worst: missing presumed dead. But that was far from the truth. After drifting for twelve days in the notoriously turbulent waters of the North Sea, without food or water and close to death with hypothermia, they were spotted by a German aircraft, who reported their position, which led to them being rescued by a vessel of the German navy.

The men gave the story that they were shipwrecked Norwegian fishermen whose boat had foundered in rough seas. There was no reason for the Germans to think otherwise, and so they were placed in a German prisoner of war camp where they remained until the end of the war. There were numerous such camps situated all over Norway.

Per Blystad, Mindor Berge and the *Sjø* – August/ September 1942

The *Sjø* was an open boat, and at 28ft long, was not particularly that big. The vessel had first arrived in Lerwick on 28 April 1942, having left Austevoll two days earlier. On board were just four people: the boat's skipper and owner, Nils Horgen, Johannes Rasmussen Kalve, Fritz Paul Nilsen, and Reidar Rasmussen.

Sometime in August or September 1942, the *Sjø* was discovered by the Germans whilst on a reconnaissance mission in Norwegian coastal waters. The two men on board were Per Blystad and Mindor Berge. Both men were captured and taken prisoner by the Germans and later shot for spying.

Anders Nærøy and the M/B *Aksel* – 8 December 1942

The 65-ft long M/B *Aksel* was the boat which made the first journey of the Shetland Bus operation on 30 August 1941. However, it had initially arrived in Shetland on 5 May 1941, with twenty Norwegian refugees desperate to escape from the German occupation of their nation. The skipper of the boat on both occasions was Anders Nærøy, but he would not be its only skipper during its time spent as part of the Shetland Bus.

On 8 December 1942, the role of being captain of the *Aksel* fell to the well-respected Norwegian skipper, Bård Grotle. The ship and its crew were on their way to Shetland from Kristiansund, a municipality on the western coast of Norway in the Nordmore district of Møre og Romsdal county. When the *Aksel* was about 200 nautical miles from Shetland, an SOS signal was received from her.

A Catalina flying boat, more commonly used during the war to spot enemy submarines, was despatched along with a motor torpedo boat to the *Aksel*'s no last known position, to search for her. The flying boat arrived on scene early the next day, at which time the *Askel*, clearly stricken, was nearly completely submerged nearby. The crew had managed to deploy their lifeboat, which was found with them in it, but the seas were too rough for the Catalina to land and carry out a rescue of the beleaguered crew. To make matters worse, due to insufficient fuel, the motor torpedo boat had returned to Lerwick before she could even get to the *Askel*'s location. By the time other aircraft and boats could get to the area to rescue the crew, the men were lost. The search went on for days, but no sign of the lifeboat or the crew was ever found. The only sensible suggestion as to the reason for the lifeboat's demise might be that it was enveloped by a rogue wave which took the crew to a watery grave.

Harold Dyb and the M/B *Sandøy* – 10 December 1942

The M/B *Sandøy* was lost on 10 December 1942, when it was attacked and sunk by a German aircraft in the North Sea, en route from Shetland to Norway. All seven of the crew were lost including 19-year-old Ole Strandokleiv.

Ola Grotle and the M/B *Feiøy* – January 1943

In January 1943, the M/B *Feiøy*, skippered by Ola Grotle, set off from Shetland on its way to Norway, but it never arrived. There are no known records of either German aircraft, submarines or ships attacking and sinking the *Feiøy*, so that leaves just two options: either it struck a mine and sank, or it sank as a result of bad weather in the North Sea. Either way, all men were lost and none of their bodies was ever recovered.

Olaf Skarpenes and the F/V *Bodø* – 1 January 1943

The fishing vessel *Bodø* left Peterhead in Scotland for Norway on 1 January 1943, as part of Operation Carhampton. On board she had a number of commandos who were to take part in the operation. Having completed her task, she left Norway on the return journey, but as she neared the Scottish coast she struck a mine and sank. All the crew were killed. One of them, Olaf Skarpenes, is commemorated on a memorial in Scalloway.

Odd Kjell Starheim and the *Tromøsund* – 28 February 1943

Odd Kjell Starheim, a Norwegian resistance fighter and agent of the SOE, was the man who came up with the original idea for Operation Carhampton, a joint British and Norwegian Special Forces plan, overseen by the SOE, which took place between January and March 1943, with the intention of capturing Nazi shipping off the west coast of German-occupied Norway.

During the German invasion of Norway in April 1940, Starheim had enlisted in the Norwegian army to fight against the Nazis. But things did not quite go according to plan and he was captured and held as a prisoner of war. Starheim was a very determined individual and soon managed to escape and make his way to neutral Sweden, but he had no plans to sit out the war in quiet comfort, it was simply part of the route he had to take to get him to Britain. But wanting to get there and physically being able to do so were two different matters. Realising he was not going to be able to make it, he returned to Norway to bide his time until he could find a way to make it across the North Sea, and to freedom. Along with two other men whom he knew and trusted, he began accumulating fuel, acquired a boat called the *Viking*, and on 11 August 1940, the three of them left the coastal town of Rauna; their destination, Scotland. Their excitement at beginning their escape was short-lived, because despite it being the height of summer, the weather in the North Sea was absolutely horrendous, so bad in fact they had to turn round and return to Rauna, where they arrived the next day. Thankfully there was an improvement in the weather, and the following day, 13 August, they set sail again, finally reaching Aberdeen on 17 August, despite having encountered yet another storm.

Starheim was one of the first men whom Captain Martin Linge selected for his newly formed Special Operations Executive's Kompani Linge. He returned to Norway on three occasions to undertake missions. In December 1940, he was taken by submarine to a point off the Norwegian coast near Farsund. He then had to make his way ashore by kayak, and on reaching the shore he carried his radio set 25 miles inland. This may not sound that demanding a task, but in the circumstances it was a sterling achievement, as not only did Starheim have to cope with the harsh Norwegian winter weather, but he was also suffering with a bad case of the flu.

The purpose of Starheim's mission was to discover what had happened to three other agents of the SOE who had previously been sent to Norway on their own mission. This was somewhat of a personal matter for Starheim, because two of the men whom he had been sent to try and locate were the same two men he had escaped from Norway with. What he, or the British authorities, did not know was that the three men Starheim had been sent to find had already been captured and executed by the Germans before he had even commenced his mission.

Starheim remained in Norway until June 1941, doing everything he could to help his fellow Norwegians, whilst at the same time causing as much disruption to the Germans as possible. He achieved most of this by being part of the Norwegian resistance and keeping in constant radio communication with the UK.

Whilst radioing a message to the SOE headquarters in Shetland, on 25 February 1941, about the German battleship *Bismarck* leaving the safety of a Norwegian fjord for the open waters of the North Sea, he became the first SOE agent to make radio contact between German-occupied Norway and the UK.

It was not long after this that Starheim realised that if he remained in his beloved Norway much longer, it was more than likely he would be captured by the Germans. With this in mind he escaped to Sweden, and from there he made his way back to the UK. But still he wanted to do more, and continue to do his best to help end the occupation of his country by the forces of Nazi Germany. On 1 January 1942, he returned to Norway, but on this occasion not with the help of a Norwegian fishing vessel, or a submarine of the Royal Navy, but by parachuting out of an aircraft of the Royal Air Force. This time he was not alone. He was accompanied by fellow SOE agent, 22-year-old, Andreas Fasting, also known by the name of Tore Lund. This was the first occasion that agents had used such a method of entering Norway.

The point of the mission was to re-establish radio communications, which had been lost, between the SOE in Shetland, and the Norwegian Resistance. This was not only a much-needed lifeline for the beleaguered Norwegians, but an extremely important link for British Intelligence. Part of the problem was the lack of information surrounding why the SOE agent in Norway had ceased his transmissions.

He had not been in Norway for long when he was captured by the dreaded Gestapo in Oslo. Whilst he was in custody being interrogated, he managed the unthinkable. Left unattended for a period of time, he somehow managed to escape from his captors, jumping from a second-storey window to escape. He managed to make radio contact with his colleagues in Shetland, who wasted no time in organising a fishing vessel to collect him and take him back to Scotland, but for a variety of reasons this failed. This meant that his options were now limited. He had made a previous escape through Sweden, but did not want to risk trying it again in case the Germans were expecting him to repeat the exercise.

Starheim's answer to his predicament was unusual to say the least, possibly even unique. He decided he would escape by hijacking a Norwegian coastal steamer, the *Galtesund*, in the small harbour at the town of Flekkefjord. Along with a small group of people, most of whom were locals also looking to escape, Starheim carried out his audacious plan and set sail on board the *Galtesund* on 15 March 1942. The group arrived in Aberdeen the following day under the cover of air support from the RAF, which had been ordered to assist.

His senior officers in the SOE were so impressed with his hijacking of the *Galtesund* that on 2 July 1942 they recommended him for the Military Cross, but when the true scale of his achievement was recognised, it was decided that he should receive the higher and more prestigious award of the DSO. The award was announced in the *London Gazette*.

Starheim was certainly an inspired individual, who always seemed to find a way to get the job done, no matter what it was he had been tasked to achieve. His ability for lateral thinking was so wide that his actions, such as the hijacking of the *Galtesund*, would rarely have been considered by other agents, his senior officers, or thankfully, the Germans.

It was as a direct result of Starheim's hijacking of the *Galtesund* that Operation Carhampton came about, which was undertaken by the SOE. The plan was to try and seize an entire German coastal shipping convoy and then bring the vessels back across the North Sea to Scotland.

Things did not get off to an auspicious start when the original plan had to be postponed in November 1942, due to inclement weather, but the operation did eventually go ahead, and involved a total of forty-one men. Thirty-one were from Kompani Linge, with a further ten men from the Royal Norwegian Navy. The first stage of the operation was a success, when the men who had been on board the Norwegian vessel, the *Bodø*, were safely landed near Abelsnes in Vest-Agder.

The operation was always going to be difficult. How a total of just forty-one men were ever going to be able to successfully board a number of ships running together in convoy, overpower the crews and then capture them all intact is unclear. Even if that were possible, they then had the even more difficult task of sailing those ships back to Scotland before the German authorities discovered what had happened and sent their aircraft after them.

The first attempt at hijacking such a convoy failed due to communication problems between the different sections of the attacking group. From there, it was downhill all the way, with the operation eventually called off. On 17 January 1943, Starheim and his colleagues tried again, but this time the outcome was even worse as they were discovered by German guards before they could even put their operation into motion. A fire-fight ensued with casualties on both sides, before the commandos managed to escape. If their presence in Norway had not been previously known about by the Germans, it certainly was after that particular interaction.

It was only because of the assistance afforded to them by local resistance fighters that they managed to evade capture by the large force of German soldiers who were hunting them. The commandos were both brave and determined, individually and as a group, and they were certainly not prepared to give up on their mission so easily.

Without making any communication with military authorities in London or any instructions to do so, the commandos decided to carry out an attack on the heavily fortified and guarded molybdenum mines at Knaben. Between 1900 and 1973, large amounts of molybdenum were mined from the surrounding mountains. This was a mineral used to strengthen steel during its production, including for military weapons of differing calibres, from rifle to large artillery pieces. Hence it was very important for the German war effort.

Despite a steely determination to succeed, it was always going to be an extremely difficult operation to carry out successfully, especially as the Germans were by then well aware of the commandos' presence in the area. Realising that any attack on the mines at Knaben was going to be unsuccessful, and likely see them incur heavy casualties, the commandos decided to cancel their entire mission. Matters were made worse when an operation approved by London, an attack on the important titanium mines at Sokndal, had to be called off due to inclement weather. Titanium can be mixed with iron, aluminium, vanadium and molybdenum, along with other elements, to produce strong, lightweight alloys that were subsequently used by the Germans for military purposes.

Starheim and his colleagues were determined not to return to the UK without having proved their worth. With this in the forefront of their thinking, they managed to hijack a Norwegian cargo steamship, the *Tromøsund*, at Rekefjord on 28 February 1943, and began their journey back to Scotland. But any success they might have achieved in successfully hijacking the *Tromøsund* came to an abrupt end when it was attacked and sunk by German aircraft, Focke Wulfe 190s, who had been alerted to its capture by enemy forces. The sinking resulted in the deaths of all of those on board, including three German prisoners of war who had been captured during the hijacking. The dead also included two passengers, twenty-six members of the crew, and the thirteen commandos, including Starheim, who had hijacked the vessel.

Out of all of those who were killed, only two bodies were ever recovered, with one of these being that of Starheim. They were both washed up on the beach at Tjorn, near Bohuslan in Sweden.

Although thirteen commandos who were part of operation were killed when the *Tromøsund* sank, another sixteen, who did not sail on her, managed to evade capture by the Germans and make their way back to England by fishing trawler, landing at West Hartlepool, on the north-east coast of England. A number of these men subsequently returned to Norway on future missions, as part of the SOE, having been transported there by vessels of the Shetland Bus.

Leif Larsen and the M/K *Bergholm* – 23 March 1943

The M/K *Bergholm* was one of the boats of the Shetland Bus operation when it was attacked by German aircraft on 23 March 1943. The vessel, which was skippered at the time by Leif Larsen, was sunk and one of the crew, 20-year-old Nils B. Vika, was killed. Larsen and the remaining six members of his crew survived. Although some of them had been wounded in the attack, they managed to row their boat to Norway, where they remained until they were able to return to Shetland on board another vessel.

Jan Sigurd Baalsrud and the *Brattholm* – 29 March 1943

During Germany's invasion of neutral Norway in 1940, one of those who fought against them was Jan Sigurd Baalsrud, who went on to become a commando in the Norwegian resistance movement, having been trained by the British in Shetland and sent back to Norway on one of the Shetland Bus vessels.

He was one of those who survived the fighting and managed to escape once Norway had surrendered. His escape route took him to Sweden, but instead of being met with open arms by a fellow neutral country, he was arrested on charges of spying, convicted of espionage and expelled from the country.

Determined to reach Britain, he took an extremely elongated route to get there. His travels took him through Russia, Africa and America, before finally arriving in Britain in 1941, where he enlisted in Kompani Linge.

The detailed account of what happened to Baalsrud and the *Brattholm* is included in the previous chapter.

The M/B *Streif* – No exact date

The M/B *Streif* was another of the vessels used as part of the Shetland Bus programme. The story of its involvement is an intriguing one, in that it shows the flexibility and quick thinking of the crew and the agents who sailed on her.

The *Streif* was sent on an operation with an agent and some supplies on board to Trondelag on the Norwegian coastline. So dedicated and determined were those on board to get the job done that they left without a navigator. The man who had been due to undertake that role had been taken ill not long before they left and there was not enough time to find a replacement. The journey from Shetland to Norway went without a hitch. The *Streif* arrived in Trondelag, dropped off the agent and the required supplies, and left. At first everything was fine, but a few hours into the return leg of the journey, without any warning the boat's engine suddenly gave out. In no time at all the *Streif* began drifting, which in the potentially hostile and unpredictable waters of the North Sea, was not a good thing. After repeated attempts at restarting the engine and after drifting aimlessly for a number of days, the crew finally managed restart the engine and get underway. However, their problem now was that they did not know where they were and therefore in which direction to head.

As if by luck, not long after managing to restart the engine, they saw a British aircraft in the skies above them, and with the use of Morse code managed to send a signal to it. Believing their position was somewhere west of Shetland and that their destination was Peterhead, they headed south after the aircraft had indicated it was heading off in an easterly direction.

After a number of hours of sailing the *Streif* ran aground on a sandbank. It was only then they realised that not only were they nowhere near Peterhead, but they had in fact arrived just off the coast of Holland. They had no time to lose, as the realisation of their situation quickly dawned on them. They knew that they would have been visible to those inland for some time, and that their greeting party was more likely going to be German than Scottish. With this in mind they quickly dumped their weapons and all other incriminating items overboard before the Germans arrived. Their story was that they had been fishing off the coast of Norway when a British vessel tried to board them and claim their boat, but they managed to escape. Fearing that their route back to Norway had been cut off, they headed out to sea and then got lost having become disorientated, and the next thing they knew was they had arrived in Holland.

Luckily their story was believed and they were detained in a prisoner of war camp, where by complete coincidence they met up with the four men from the *Frøya* who had been bobbing around in the North Sea on the raft made out of oil drums.

Either the crew of the *Streif* were good liars, or even better story tellers, or the Germans who had discovered them were rather gullible. The alternative outcome for the crew of the *Streif* would have undoubtedly seen them being shot as spies.

Submarine Chasers

In the submarine chasers, a return journey from Shetland to a destination on the west coast of Norway, of which there were many, could be as quick as leave Shetland one day and return by the end of the following day, but they could also be as long as two to four days. It really depended on whether the boat had to stay in Norway whilst it waited for a returning agent or a refugee to arrive at the pick-up point. Waiting for too long was not really a preferred option of the boats' skippers and crews.

I only fully appreciated the dedication and bravery of the men who crewed these original Shetland Bus boats when I saw a photograph of one of them fighting its way through the unpredictable waters of the North Sea, next to the photograph of one of the more powerful American submarine chasers, which came into use in October 1943. A comparison of how much of an improvement the submarine chasers were would be to change from a First World War four-winged aircraft, to that of a Second World War Spitfire.

In Closing

Although the names of many of those who were involved in the Shetland Bus operations have been well documented, there are undoubtedly many who were not. It would be fair to say that the route known as the Shetland Bus worked on many different levels, with its origins not coming out of military necessity, but from Norwegian ingenuity and steely determination.

Because of the inherent dangers of making such a journey, at any time of the year, the individuals who made them were incredibly brave. When I say them, I mean the captains of the boats, their crews, and the refugees who deemed it necessary for them to have to leave their country and homes behind, and to escape the evil tyranny of German occupation and the dangers that went with it.

For some it was a desire, whilst for others it was because the Germans, which in most cases usually meant the Gestapo, were either already after them, or hot on their heels. For the latter of those two groups, there really was only one decision to make, and that was to get out of the country as quickly as possible, the safety aspect of how they did that, does not appear to have been that high on their agenda.

Appendix I: Norwegians Who Died Whilst in Service of the Shetland Bus

The following list, in no particular order, names those Norwegians who died whilst in service with the Shetland Bus. Alongside their name is the year of their death and the name of the vessel they were on at the time.

- Mils I. Nesse, 23 years, 1941, *Siglaos*
- Karsten Sangolt, 28 years, 1941, *Arthur*
- Ingvald Lerøy, 21 years, 1941, *Blia*
- Birger O. Bjørnsen, 21 years, 1941, *Blia*
- Sven Eagerld, 27 years, 1941, *Blia*
- Olav Kvakhelm, 25 years, 1941, *Blia*
- Arne O. Leroy, 21 years, 141, *Blia*
- Odd M. Svinoy, 18 years, 1941, *Blia*
- Ole Okland, 23 years, 1941, *Blia*
- Per Blystad, 31 years, 1942, *Sjø*
- Mindor Berge, 25 years, 1942, *Sjø*
- Harald Dyb, 25 years, 1942, *Sandøy*
- Arthur Byrknes, 25 years, 1942 *Sandøy*
- Nils Horgen, 27 years, 1942, *Sandøy*
- Olav L. Kinn, 27 years, 1942, *Sandøy*
- OLav Melkevik, 28 years, 1942, *Sandøy*
- Ole Strandokliev, 19 years, 1942, *Sandøy*

- Kare Stobakvik, 21 years, 1942, *Sandøy*
- Bård O. Grotle, 25 years, 1942, *Aksel*
- Schander Berg, 26 years, 1942, *Aksel*
- Ivar L. Brekke, 21 years, 1942, *Aksel*
- Tore Froysa, 26 years, 1942, *Aksel*
- John Lodden, 26 years, 1942, *Aksel*
- Ove Allen, 21 years, 1942, *Aksel*
- Olav Skarpenes, 49 years, *Bodø*
- Ola Grotle, 27 years, 1943, *Feiøy*
- Indreas Geiteroy, 23 years, 1943, *Feiøy*
- Ulf T. V. Johansen, 25 years, 1943, *Feiøy*
- Johan Kilingreset, 27 years, 1943, *Feiøy*
- Harald Novoy, 20 years, 1943, *Feiøy*
- Walter Olsen, 23 years, 1943, *Feiøy*
- Roald Strand, 25 years, 1943, *Feiøy*
- Hans H. Ovretveit, 23 years, 1943, *Feiøy*
- Nils B. Vika, 20 years, 1943, *Bergholm*
- Sverre Kverhellen, 36 years, 1943, *Brattholm*
- Bjorn N. Bolstad, 21 years, 1943, *Brattholm*
- Frithjof M. Haugland, 26 years, 1943, *Brattholm*
- Magnus J. Kvalvik, 29 years, 1943, *Brattholm*
- Erik Reichelt, 25 years, 1943, *Brattholm*
- Harold Bratvik, 25 years, 1943, *Brattholm*
- Sjur O. Trovag, 36 years, 1943, *Brattholm*
- Alfred Vik, 23 years, 1943, *Brattholm*
- Peder K. Nonas, 18 years, *Boating Accident*
- Ragnar E. Sandoy, 32 years, *Boating Accident*

Appendix II: Norwegian Vessels

The following is a list of Norwegian, mainly fishing, vessels, which made it out of Norway during the course of the Second World War. This information has been gleaned from the website www. warsailors.com, and although some of the boats became part of the Shetland Bus programme, not all of them did. But these still arrived in Shetland from different locations along the coastline of Norway, carrying Norwegian refugees who wanted to escape their country. If I have already written about some of these boats elsewhere in this chapter, I will not include them again here.

- *Albatros*, first arrived Scotland 5 September 1941.
- M/B *Alf*, first arrived in Scotland on 18 September 1941.
- M/S *Andholmen*, first arrived in Scotland on about 11 June 1940.
- M/B *Anna*, first arrived in Scotland on 19 January 1942.
- M/B *Arnafjord*, first arrived in Scotland on 29 September 1941.
- M/B *Aron*, first arrived Scotland on 18 March 1941.
- M/B *Bjorg*, first arrived in Scotland on 7 August 1941.
- M/B *Bob*, first arrived in Scotland on 23 July 1941.
- M/B *Borgchild*, first arrived in Scotland on 6 September 1941.
- M/B *Breisund*, is somewhat of a strange story because on 28 May 1940, it arrived off Haroldswick, in Shetland, having left Norway two days earlier, but it was lost to the seas and never actually landed. All crew and passengers, which included five British soldiers, were saved.

- M/B *Buestein*, first arrived in Scotland on 22 November 1941.
- M/B *Bofjord*, first arrived in Scotland on 10 June 1941.
- M/B *Bovag*, first arrived in Scotland on 2 April 1941.
- M/B *Cathinka II*, first arrived in Scotland on 19 August 1941.
- M/B *Dimant*, first arrived in Scotland on 2 November 1941.
- M/B *Dolsey*, first arrived in Scotland on 18 April 1941.
- M/B *Dronning Maud*, first arrived in Scotland on 20 August 1941.
- M/B *Drott*, first arrived in Scotland on 19 September 1941.
- M/B *Duen*, first arrived in Scotland on 25 October 1941.
- M/B *Eli*, first arrived in Scotland on 6 January 1942.
- M/B *Elida*, first arrived in Scotland on 29 March 1945.
- M/B *Elieser*, first arrived in Scotland on 4 September 1941.
- M/K *Enos*, first arrived in Scotland on 26 March 1941.
- M/S *Erkna*, first arrived in Scotland on 19 November 1941.
- M/B *Erling*, first arrived in Scotland on 31 August 1941.
- M/L *Eva*, first arrived in Scotland on 31 August 1941.
- M/B *Farmann*, first arrived in Scotland on 28 August 1941.
- M/B *Feie*, first arrived in Scotland on 1 October 1941.
- M/B *Fernanda*, first arrived in Scotland on 23 September 1941.
- M/B *Fiskaren*, first arrived in Scotland on 3 October 1941.
- M/B *Fisken*, first arrived in Scotland on 13 August 1941.
- M/B *Fiskergutten*, first arrived in Scotland on 21 April 1940.
- M/B *Flink*, first arrived in Scotland on 10 August 1941.
- M/S *Flink*, first arrived in Scotland on 17 May 1940.
- M/B *Forsak*, first arrived in Scotland on 9 May 1941.
- M/B *Forsak*, although it has the same name of the vessel above, it is a different vessel, which first arrived in Scotland on 29 July 1942.
- M/B *Fram*, first arrived in Scotland on 1 May 1942.
- M/B *Fred*, first arrived in Scotland on 4 October 1941.
- M/B *Fremad II*, first arrived in Scotland on 6 October 1941.
- M/B *Fri*, first arrived in Scotland on 26 October 1941.

- M/B *Fri*, but a different boat to the one mentioned above, first arrived in Sunderland on 6 October 1941.
- M/B *Frimann*, first arrived in Scotland on 17 February 1941.
- M/B *Fritjof Wiese*, first arrived in Scotland on 23 October 1941.
- M/B *Gangar*, first arrived in Scotland on 16 May 1944.
- M/B *Glimt*, first arrived in Scotland on 1 June 1941.
- M/B *Gneist*, first arrived Scotland on 12 June 1940.
- M/B *Gullborg*, first arrived in Scotland on 23 September 1941.
- M/B *Hallkjell*, first arrived in Scotland on 6 April 1941.
- M/K *Harald II*, first arrived in Scotland on 10 June 1941.
- M/B *Haugen*, first arrived in Scotland on 27 October 1941.
- M/B *Haugland*, first arrived in Scotland on 29 November 1941.
- M/B *Havlyn*, first arrived in Scotland on 20 October 1940.
- M/B *Havtor*, first arrived in Scotland on 9 March 1941.
- M/B *Havoy I*, first arrived in Scotland on 9 March 1945.
- M/B *Heimfjell*, first arrived in Scotland on 14 March 1941.
- M/B *Heimly*, first arrived in Scotland on 13 April 1945.
- M/B *Herny*, first arrived in Scotland on 8 July 1941.
- M/B *Hitsoy*, first arrived in Scotland on 29 August 1941.
- M/B *Hjas*, first arrived in Scotland on 2 September 1944.
- M/B *Hugin (M 54 U)*, first arrived in Scotland on 17 August 1941.
- M/B *Hadyr*, first arrived in Scotland on 22 September 1941.
- M/B *Hapet*, first arrived in Scotland on 3 August 1941.
- M/B *Igland*, first arrived in Scotland on 25 December 1940.
- M/B *Ingleborg (H 6 S)*, first arrived in Scotland on 22 July 1941.
- M/B *Ingleborg (SF 224 SU)*, first arrived in Scotland on 19 August 1941.
- M/B *Irene*, first arrived in Scotland on 4 August 1941.
- M/B *I Win*, first arrived in Scotland on 30 October 1944.

- M/B *Jakk*, first arrived in Scotland on 10 September 1941.
- M/B *Jan*, first arrived in Scotland on 7 October 1941.
- R/S *Johan Bruusgaard*, first arrived in Scotland on 19 March 1945.
- M/B *Jabaek*, first arrived in Scotland on 4 May 1940.
- M/B *Kari*, first arrived in Scotland on 30 May 1943.
- M/B *Klebb*, first arrived in Scotland on 1 September 1941.
- M/B *Klippen*, first arrived in Scotland on 26 August 1941.
- M/B *Kolbjorn*, first arrived in Scotland on 23 August 1941.
- M/B *Kvalen*, first arrived in Scotland on 3 October 1941.
- M/B *Kvikk*, first arrived in Scotland on 21 February 1941.
- Sailboat *Lady Nancy*, first arrived in England on 3 June 1940.
- M/S *Laila*, first arrived in Scotland on 9 April 1942.
- M/S *Laugen*, first arrived in Scotland on 17 August 1941.
- M/S *Leda*, first arrived in Scotland on 4 September 1941.
- M/S *Leiv*, first arrived in Scotland in May 1940.
- M/S *Lilly*, first arrived in Scotland on 27 August 1941.
- M/B *Lindesnes*, first arrived in Scotland on 19 February 1941.
- M/S *Lindoy*, first arrived in Scotland on 12 August 1941.
- M/S *Liv*, first arrived in Scotland on 23 April 1941.
- M/B *Livlig*, first arrived in Scotland on 30 May 1940.
- M/B *Lom*, first arrived in Scotland on 12 July 1944.
- M/B *Loyal*, first arrived in Scotland in August 1941.
- M/G *Lur*, first arrived in Scotland on 19 May 1941.
- M/S *Lygrefjord*, first arrived in Scotland on 28 August 1941.
- M/B *Lyn*, first arrived in Scotland on 13 April 1945.
- M/B *Lyrnes*, first arrived in Scotland on 29 August 1941.
- M/B *Margot*, first arrived in Scotland on 17 September 1941.
- M/B *Merkur*, first arrived in Scotland on 22 March 1941.
- M/B *Midtoy*, first arrived in Scotland on 10 October 1941.
- M/B *Motig*, first arrived in Scotland on 11 February 1941.
- M/B *Nils*, first arrived in Scotland on 19 September 1941.

- M/S *Njord*, first arrived in Scotland on 17 September 1941.
- M/B *Njal*, first arrived in Scotland on 1 April 1941.
- M/B *Nor*, first arrived in Scotland on 8 October 1941.
- M/B *Nora*, first arrived in Scotland on 15 October 1941.
- M/B *Nordhay*, first arrived in Scotland on 30 May 1941.
- M/B *Nordkynn*, first arrived in Scotland on 8 June 1941.
- M/S *Nordlys*, first arrived Scotland on 7 July 1940.
- M/B *Nordnes*, first arrived Scotland on 21 January 1941.
- M/S *Nordsjøen*, first arrived in Scotland on 5 August 1941.
- M/B *Norseman*, first arrived in Scotland on 10 October 1941.
- M/B *Notbas*, first arrived in Scotland on 4 May 1941.
- M/B *Notmann*, first arrived in Scotland on 16 August 1941.
- M/B *Nyken*, first arrived in Scotland on 28 May 1940.
- M/B *Nyo*, first arrived in Scotland at the end of May, beginning of June 1940.
- M/S *Odin*, first arrived in Scotland on 9 September 1941.
- M/S *Olaf*, first arrived in Scotland on 3 July 1941.
- M/B *Olaf*, first arrived in Scotland on 16 March 1941.
- M/B *Olaf II*, first arrived in Scotland on 6 June 1941.
- M/B *Olaf (M73V)*, first arrived in Scotland on 30 September 1941.
- M/B *Olai*, first arrived in Scotland on 17 August 1941.
- M/B *Ottar*, first arrived in England on 19 September 1941.
- M/B *Pluggen*, first arrived in Scotland on 26 July 1940.
- M/B *Pokal*, first arrived in Scotland on 7 November 1940.
- M/S *Porat*, first arrived in Scotland on 9 May 1940.
- M/B *Reidar*, first arrived in Scotland on 8 January 1943.
- M/S *Rival*, first arrived in Scotland on 8 September 1941.
- L/S *Rundo*, first arrived in Scotland on 21 October 1941.
- M/K *Rupee*, first arrived in Scotland on 14 February 1942.
- M/S *Rypa*, first arrived in Scotland on 16 January 1941.
- M/B *Sandvikhorn*, first arrived in Scotland on 9 May 1940.
- M/B *Set*, first arrived in Scotland on 25 July 1941.

- M/B *Signal*, first arrived in Scotland in May 1941.
- M/B *Signal*, first arrived in Scotland on 14 July 1944.
- M/B *Sigurd*, first arrived in Scotland on 16 March 1941.
- M/B *Silden*, first arrived in Scotland on 15 October 1941.
- M/S *Sjoblomsten*, first arrived in Scotland on 24 June 1941.
- M/B *Sjoblomsten (M 60 HO)*, first arrived in Scotland on 27 April 1941.
- M/B *Sjoblomsten (SF 45 B)*, first arrived in Scotland on 11 March 1941.
- M/B *Sjoglimt*, first arrived in Scotland in June 1940.
- M/B *Sjogutt*, first arrived in Scotland on 13 July 1941.
- M/B *Sjogutten*, first arrived in Scotland in May 1940.
- M/S *Sjoleik*, first arrived in Scotland on 13 October 1941.
- M/B *Sjolivet*, first arrived in Scotland on 23 September 1941.
- M/B *Sjolyst*, first arrived in Scotland on 1 November 1941.
- M/B *Skarv*, first arrived in Scotland on 6 June 1941.
- M/B *Skjaergard*, first arrived in Scotland on 6 October 1941.
- M/B *Sleipner*, first arrived in Scotland on 19 October 1941.
- M/S *Slotteroy*, first arrived in Scotland on 7 June 1940.
- M/B *Smart*, first arrived in Scotland on 12 August 1942.
- M/B *Snedig*, first arrived in Scotland on 17 August 1944.
- M/B *Snal*, first arrived in Scotland on 20 May 1940.
- M/S *Solhaug*, first arrived in Scotland on 15 September 1941.
- M/B *Solid*, first arrived in Scotland on 7 August 1941.
- M/B *Solrenning*, first arrived in Scotland on 6 September 1941.
- M/B *Solveig*, first arrived in Scotland on 25 August 1941.
- M/B *Soloy*, first arrived in Scotland on 4 August 1941.
- M/B *Stanley*, first arrived in Scotland on 25 September 1941.
- M/B *Start*, first arrived in Scotland on 18 June 1944.
- M/S *Steinborg*, first arrived in Scotland on 24 September 1941.

- M/S *Straumoy*, first arrived in Scotland on 2 September 1941.
- M/B *Stolsgut*, first arrived in Scotland on 5 October 1941.
- M/S *Stal I*, first arrived in Scotland on 8 September 1941.
- M/K *Sund I*, first arrived in Scotland on 25 September 1941.
- M/S *Svalen (SF 106 A)*, first arrived in Scotland on 27 May 1940.
- M/S *Svalen (N 17 TN)*, first arrived in Scotland on 22 September 1942.
- M/B *Svanen*, first arrived in Scotland on 15 August 1941.
- M/B *Svanen II,* first arrived in Scotland on 30 August 1941.
- M/S *Svanen III*, first arrived in Scotland on 21 August 1941.
- M/B *Sverre*, first arrived in Scotland on 1 April 1941.
- M/B *Sylvia*, first arrived in Scotland on 17 April 1941.
- M/B *Tassen*, first arrived in England on 14 September 1941.
- M/B *Telma*, first arrived in Scotland on 30 October 1941.
- M/B *Traust*, first arrived in Scotland sometime in July 1940.
- M/B *Trygg*, first arrived in Scotland on 24 October 1940.
- M/B *Trygve*, first arrived in Scotland on 4 January 1942.
- M/B *Ulabrand*, first arrived in Scotland on 19 March 1941.
- M/B *Ulf*, first arrived in Scotland on 8 December 1940.
- M/B *Ulstein*, first arrived in Scotland on 24 June 1941.
- M/S *Utnoring*, first arrived in Scotland on 30 September 1941.
- M/B *Valder (SF 57 K)*, first arrived in Scotland on 16 August 1941.
- M/B *Valder (M 9 V)*, first arrived in Scotland on 7 April 1941.
- M/S *Vega*, first arrived in Scotland on 22 May 1940.
- M/B *Veslemoy*, first arrived in Scotland on 8 October 1941.
- M/B *Vest*, first arrived in Scotland on 18 May 1940.
- M/B *Vestern*, first arrived in Scotland on 9 May 1940.
- M/B *Veststein*, first arrived in Scotland on 6 May 1940.
- M/B *Veten*, first arrived in Scotland on 12 September 1940.

- M/B *Victory*, first arrived in Scotland on 11 August 1941.
- M/B *Viken*, first arrived in Scotland on 12 March 1941.
- M/S *Viking*, first arrived in Scotland on 12 August 1941.
- M/B *Viking*, first arrived in Scotland on 17 August 1941.
- M/K *Vikingen*, first arrived in Scotland on 31 August 1941.
- M/B *Vikingen II*, first arrived in Scotland on 11 September 1941.
- Pilot Vessel *Villa II*, first arrived in Scotland on 23 August 1941.
- M/B *Viola*, first arrived in Scotland on 15 September 1941.
- M/B *Volga*, first arrived in Scotland on 9 March 1941.
- M/S *Von*, first arrived in Scotland on 14 October 1941.
- M/B *Von*, first arrived in Scotland on 4 January 1941.
- M/B *Vagsfjord*, first arrived in Scotland on 4 January 1941.
- M/B *Wailet*, first arrived in Scotland on 11 May 1940.
- M/B *Wiken*, first arrived in Scotland on 12 March 1941.

In addition to the above vessels, there were a number of others that left Norway, but ended up, whether by intention or otherwise, in other locations, such as the Faroe Islands, Iceland and even Canada. There were also a number of boats who, having left Norway, never arrived in Scotland, and were never heard of again. Most of these boats were lost due to nothing more sinister than very bad weather, but there were those who may have struck mines or been sunk as a result of engagement with either German aircraft, naval vessels or submarines.

Those who made these journeys did so knowing full well the risks they were taking, for both themselves and their families. Some of the early crossings involved entire families, including women and very young children. After the British defeat in Norway, many British soldiers made their way back to the UK on board Norwegian fishing vessels.

Appendix III: Hansard UK Parliamentary Reports

The following is a question that was asked in the House of Commons on 24 April 1940, by Captain Leonard Frank Plugge, in relation to the German treatment of the civilian population of Norway since the time of their invasion and subsequent occupation of the country.

Captain Plugge, who besides being a radio entrepreneur and a Conservative MP, served during the First World War. Initially he became a member of the Royal Naval Volunteer Reserve, but in 1918 transferred to the newly formed Royal Air Force, where he rose to the rank of captain, and remained until 1921.

Before the First World War he had gained a BSc degree in civil engineering, and on leaving the RAF in 1921, he was elected as a Fellow of the Royal Aeronautical Society. He later became interested in politics and in the 1935 General Election was elected MP for Chatham in Kent, when he defeated prospective Labour candidate, Hugh Gaitskell, by a majority of 5,897 votes.

Captain Plugge asked about reports he had received indicating that German forces had been shooting civilians in Norway.

Mr Rab Butler, Conservative MP for Saffron Walden, answering on behalf of the prime minister, gave the following reply.

It appears from the official German broadcasts of 12th, 13th and 19th April that the German command in Oslo have declared that any persons found fighting the German forces will be treated as *franc-tireurs* and shot, and that some persons have already been shot on this ground.

They have also declared that every civilian met carrying arms or committing any act of sabotage will be shot on the spot. They have in addition admitted that they have forced Norwegian civilians to drive German soldiers into the firing line in commandeered cars. Comment on such methods of war is superfluous, but I am glad to have this opportunity of making the facts known.

Butler was an interesting character. He was no great lover of Churchill and was one of those who did not want him to become prime minister, instead favouring Lord Halifax for the position. He was also one of those interested in the possibility of reaching a compromised peace agreement with Hitler.

An example of Butler's attitude to the war could be seen in what became known as the Prytz Affair. On 17 June 1940, just a matter of days after the fall of Paris to Nazi Germany, Butler had an unofficial meeting at St James's Park with the Swedish trade envoy Dr Bjorn Prytz. Sweden was of course a neutral nation throughout the course of the Second World War. The meeting continued, albeit briefly, in the Foreign Office. During this time, Butler even went as far as conferring with Lord Halifax in his office. At best Butler's conduct was somewhat naïve, at worst it was borderline treasonable.

Prytz reported back to his government colleagues in Stockholm that Butler had declared that British policy 'must be determined by common sense and not bravado'. Prytz added that 'he had assured me that no opportunity for reaching a compromised peace would be neglected if the possibility were offered on reasonable conditions.'

Understandably, Churchill was absolutely furious when he heard of Butler's unofficial and unsupported actions.

Mr George Strauss, Labour MP for Lambeth North asked:

Has he any information concerning the approval given by the Norwegian Government to Herr Christensen on his action in accepting the chairmanship of the committee for the administration of Norwegian territory under German occupation; and will he make a statement?

Mr Rab Butler:

The position of the administrative council in Oslo under the chairmanship of Mr Christensen has been made clear by a proclamation issued on 17th April by the King of Norway in Council.

On 2 May 1940, Clement Atlee, the MP for Stepney and Limehouse, and leader of the Labour Party, asked the following question in the House of Commons:

Is the Prime Minister now able to make a statement on the position in Norway?

The prime minister was indeed able to provide the House with a detailed and thorough update of the situation in Norway:

I should like first to thank the House for their indulgence in not pressing me to make a statement earlier in the week upon the operations in Norway. I know how many must have been longing for news even of the most meagre description, but Hon. Members have realised the difficulty of making any such statement without disclosing information which would have been of value to the enemy, and they have refrained from asking those questions to which they and the country have naturally been so anxious to obtain an answer. I am afraid I must ask them to exercise their patience a little longer before I can give them a full story, for it is impossible to make public as yet plans and movements which are not complete.

I can, therefore, only make an interim statement today but I hope that the First Lord of the Admiralty and I may be able to say a good deal more early next week when, no doubt, the House will desire to debate the whole subject in the light of the information before them.

The House will, of course, remember that some three months ago we had made preparations for the despatch of an Allied force to the assistance of Finland. The possibility of reaching Finland was dependent upon the collaboration of the governments of Norway and Sweden and, realising that even their acquiescence in the passage of Allied troops might involve them in an invasion by Germany, we prepared other forces to go to their assistance in that contingency. It did not escape our attention that in such a case Trondheim and other western ports of Norway as well as the aerodrome at Stavanger might well be the subject of attack by Germany, and accordingly further forces again were made ready to occupy these places. I should, however, make it clear that the instructions to the commanders of these forces provided that they were only to proceed to the occupation in one of two conditions: either that they were invited to do so by the Norwegian government, or that Norwegian neutrality had already been violated.

The House is aware that permission to send troops to Finland through Norway and Sweden was refused; and, after a certain period, the greater part of the forces which had been accumulated were dispersed, since both they and the ships which were allocated for their transport were wanted elsewhere. About a month ago, however, it was decided that certain small forces should be kept in readiness to occupy Norwegian Western ports at short notice, in case of an act of aggression by Germany against South Norway. It will be noted again that any action contemplated by us on Norwegian soil was conditional upon prior violation of Norwegian neutrality by Germany.

It has been asked how it was that, in spite of these preparations, Germany was able to forestall us. The answer is simple. It was by long-planned, carefully-elaborated treachery against an unsuspecting and almost unarmed people. We had been aware for many months that the Germans were accumulating transports and troops in Baltic ports, and that these troops were constantly being practised in embarkation and disembarkation. It was evident that some act of aggression was in contemplation, but these forces were equally available for attack upon Finland, Sweden, Norway, Holland, or this country, and it was impossible to tell beforehand where the blow would fall. If we had known that Denmark and Norway were to be the victims, we could not have prevented what happened, without the co-operation of those countries. But, in the belief that their neutrality would save them, they took no precautions, and they gave us no warning of an attack, which, indeed, they never suspected.

It will be remembered that in the early days of April, His Majesty's government decided that they could no longer tolerate the continued use of Norwegian territorial waters as a long communication trench by which Germany could obtain constant supplies of iron ore and other contraband, and they had decided that on 8th April minefields would be laid at three points within Norwegian territorial waters, which would force this traffic out on to the high seas, where it could be intercepted. It is a curious chance that this date of 8th April, decided upon by His Majesty's government for this minor operation, should have coincided almost exactly with that chosen by the German government for their long-prepared invasion of Norway.

The Norwegian campaign opened on Sunday, 7th April, when we got information that a large German naval force was moving towards and along the West Coast of Norway. That evening the main Battle Fleet and the Second Cruiser Squadron sailed from Scapa and Rosyth in the hope of engaging the enemy. On Monday, 8th April, the First Cruiser Squadron sailed to join in the operations. On the morning of 9th April German land forces entered Denmark, and, aided by internal treachery, prepared long beforehand, naval forces seized and landed troops at Oslo, Stavanger, Bergen and Trondheim.

On the same day His Majesty's Ship *Renown*, which was accompanying the destroyers watching over the minefield near Narvik, engaged the German battle cruiser *Scharnhorst* off the Northern coast of Norway opposite Narvik in extremely bad weather conditions and low visibility, inflicting considerable damage, although full reports of this were not available until the 11th. In the meantime, our destroyers had discovered a number of enemy vessels which had entered the Narvik Fjord under cover of a snowstorm, and on the next day they fought the action in which their gallant Commander, Captain Warburton Lee, lost his life, and other losses were sustained, but in which heavy damage was inflicted on the German destroyers and the merchant vessels in the Fjord.

In view of the obscurity of the situation in Central Norway and the importance of securing Narvik, our first military forces, which we had promptly assembled, sailed direct to the Narvik area, arriving there on 15th April. In the meantime, the very successful naval attack on 13th April completely destroyed the enemy's naval forces at that port, and made it unnecessary to utilise for the capture of Narvik all the forces originally earmarked for that operation.

In deciding upon our further action, the objectives which we had in view were: first, to give all the support and assistance in our power to the Norwegians; second, to resist or delay the German advance from the South; and, third, to facilitate the rescue and protection of the Norwegian King and government. It was obvious that these objectives could be most speedily attained if it were possible to capture Trondheim, and, in spite of the hazardous nature of the operation, with the Germans in possession of the place and in occupation of the only really efficient aerodrome in South-West Norway, at Stavanger, we resolved to make the effort. Since any landing would probably be opposed, it was essential that the first contingents should go as light as possible, to secure bases to which the heavier equipment could subsequently be transported, and two landing places were selected, respectively North and South of Trondheim.

At Namsos in the North, naval forces landed on 14th April and were followed by British troops on the 16–18th. A few days later, the French Chasseurs Alpins landed, and the arrival of these staunch and experienced troops was a welcome support to our men. Part of this force advanced rapidly to the neighbourhood of Steinkjer to support the Norwegians who were known to be holding that place. South of Trondheim, the naval party landed at Andalsnes on 17th April, followed by troops on 18th and 19th April. These advanced to the important railway junction of Dombaas, and a contingent went on to the South and joined the Norwegians who were opposing at Lillehammer the main German advance from the South.

I cannot today give any details of the fighting which has taken place on both fronts since the landing took place. All that can be said at present is that our troops fought with gallantry and determination, and inflicted heavy losses upon the enemy. Nevertheless, the Allied forces in these regions were faced, as we had realised that they would be faced, with serious difficulties. Foremost among these was the fact that the available aerodromes were already in enemy hands. The most effective defence against air attack, the use of fighter aircraft, was thus largely denied to us, and any hon. Members who have suffered the experience of being bombed from the air by low-flying aeroplanes will know how greatly the supply and movement of troops are hampered.

In the circumstances, it became evident to us some days ago that it would be impossible, owing to the German local air superiority, to land the artillery and tanks which would be necessary in order to enable our troops to withstand the enemy drive from the South. It must be remembered that, in spite of the magnificent work by British submarines and a French flotilla in the Skaggerack and the unceasing efforts of the Royal Air Force, particularly in bombing the aerodromes at Aalborg, in Denmark, the starting point, and Oslo, the landing place, of German troop carriers, it has always been possible for the Germans, with their usual disregard of life, even of their own people, to send reinforcements to Norway at a much greater rate than would be open to us with the inadequate landing places that we have to rely on.

Accordingly, we decided last week that we must abandon any idea of taking Trondheim from the South and that we must, therefore, withdraw our troops from that area and transfer them elsewhere. The operation of withdrawal in face of the enemy is one which has always been recognised as among the most delicate and difficult of military operations, and the action of Sir John Moore at Corunna, though accompanied by heavy loss of life, including the Commander, has taken its place among the classic examples of British military skill. In the present instance, we have been more fortunate. Thanks to the powerful forces which the navy was able to bring to bear and the determination and skilful dispositions of General Paget, in command of the British land forces in the area, backed by the splendid courage and tenacity of the troops, we have now withdrawn the whole of our forces from Andalsnes under the very noses of the German aeroplanes, without, as far as I am aware, losing a single man in this operation. I should like to express my profound admiration for the manner in which all ranks have performed their tasks in the area South of Trondheim. I cannot yet give the House particulars of the casualties which our forces have sustained in the various operations, but I hope, and I have some reason to believe, that they have not been heavy in proportion to the scale of operations. I expect that we shall be able to get more detailed reports before long, and I trust that this most distressing but inevitable period of uncertainty may not be prolonged. Although in the face of the overwhelming difficulties of the situation, it has not been possible to effect the capture of the town, I am satisfied that the balance of advantage lies up to the present with the Allied Forces.

It may be useful if I examine this point in somewhat greater detail. I have no doubt that the Germans expected a walk-over in Norway, as in Denmark. That expectation has been frustrated by the courage of the Norwegian people and by the efforts of the Allies. After three weeks of war, in which heavy losses have been sustained by the enemy on the sea, on land and in the air, Norway is not conquered, while the considerable supplies of ore which Germany was formerly obtaining from Narvik have been indefinitely suspended. During the period of just over three weeks the German naval losses amount to a serious figure. They include two capital ships damaged, certainly three, possibly four, cruisers sunk, eleven destroyers sunk, and five U-boats sunk. Thirty transports and store ships have been sunk, scuttled, or set on fire, with a loss of several thousands of lives. A further ten transport or store ships have been struck by our torpedoes and probably sunk.

The losses sustained by the Royal Navy in the same period are: Four destroyers, three submarines, one sloop and five trawlers sunk. Five other warships have been damaged by air attack, and one store ship has also been sunk by U-boat torpedo. It will be seen from these figures that, whereas the strength and efficiency of the Royal Navy have been little, if at all, affected, the injury to the German navy has been so substantial as to alter the entire balance of naval power, and to permit an important re-distribution of the main Allied fleets. In this connection, I might mention that it has been thought possible to revert to the more normal distribution of ships in the Mediterranean, which has for some time been affected by our requirements in the North Sea. A British and French battle fleet, with cruisers and ancillary craft, is already in the Eastern basin of the Mediterranean on its way to Alexandria.

Returning to the Norway campaign, the German losses in men, whether from the sinking of war vessels, from the destruction of transports or in the course of the fighting in Norway itself on land and in the air, cannot be estimated with any accuracy, but they must have amounted to many thousands. At this moment, I would say to any who may be drawing hasty conclusions from the fact that for the present we have not succeeded in taking Trondheim, it is far too soon to strike the Norwegian balance-sheet yet, for the campaign has merely concluded a single phase in which it is safe to say that if we have not achieved our objective, neither have the Germans achieved theirs, while their losses are far greater than ours.

But I would take this opportunity of addressing a warning both to this House and to the country. We have no intention of allowing Norway to become merely a side show, but neither are we going to be trapped into such a dispersal of our forces as would leave us dangerously weak at the vital centre. We know that our enemy hold a central position. They have immense forces always mounted ready for attack, and the attack can be launched with lightning rapidity in any one of many fields. We know that they are prepared, and would not scruple, to invade Holland, or Belgium, or both. Or it may be that their savage hordes will be hurled against their innocent neighbours in the South-East of Europe. They might well do more than one of these things in preparation for an attempt at a large-scale attack on the Western Front or even a lightning swoop on this country. It would be foolish indeed to reveal to the enemy our conception of the strategy best calculated to secure their defeat. But this can be said, for it is obvious that we must not so disperse or tie up our forces as to weaken our freedom of action in vital emergencies which may at any moment arise. We must seize every chance, as we have done and shall continue to do in Norway, to inflict damage upon the enemy, but we must not allow ourselves to forget the long-term strategy which will win the war.

Mr. Speaker, let me repeat that what I have said is only an interim statement. Certain operations are in progress, and we must do nothing which might jeopardise the lives of those engaged in them. I would, therefore, ask the House to defer comment and question until we can have the Debate next week, when I anticipate that that particular difficulty will not arise.

Mr Clement Attlee:

In normal conditions, in view of the very important statement that the Prime Minister has made, one would have liked to have had a full discussion in this House on the issues which are raised, but the safety of our men must be the paramount consideration, and the Prime Minister has said that an opportunity will be afforded for a wider discussion next week. In those circumstances I think it would be inadvisable and wrong for me to put any Supplementary Questions to the Prime Minister.

Sir Archibald Sinclair, MP for Caithness and Sutherland, and Leader of the Liberal Party:

While my honourable Friends and I are grateful to the Prime Minister for the statement which he has made today, for which the House and the country have been

anxiously awaiting, I agree with him that it would be
inadvisable to have a discussion today. I am glad that
he has given us this assurance, that we shall have an
opportunity to do so at a very early stage. May I only say
this before I sit down, that I hope we shall have more than
one day's Debate? I am quite sure that there are Members
in all parts of the House who will want to take part in
the Debate, which must not be one which is confined to
a few leading speakers. Therefore, I hope there will be
ample opportunity for Members of the rank and file in
all parts of the House.

The Prime Minister:

I shall be quite prepared to discuss the suggestion which
the right hon. Gentleman has made, through the usual
channels.

On 17 June 1941, a brief exchange took place in the House of
Commons between two men with military experience Captain
(Later Sir) Richard Pilkington, the Conservative MP for Widnes,
who had previously served with the Coldstream Guards in the
Sudan and Egypt, and who had relinquished his commission in
1935 to go into politics.

On the outbreak of the Second World War, he re-enlisted in
the army and travelled to France with the British Expeditionary
Force. He was awarded the Military Cross after he returned to
England with one of the last groups that managed to escape from
Dunkirk in 1940. He left the army again in 1942, becoming a Civil
Lord of the Admiralty, and led naval missions to Burma, Ceylon
and India.

The other individual was Captain Henry David Reginald
Margesson, who was the Conservative MP for Upton, near Westham
in the East End of London, and the Secretary of State for War.

Captain Pilkington asked the Secretary of State for War whether he had any information as to how many French troops were sent to Norway in April and May 1940 and was told by Margesson that the total strength of the French troops sent to Norway was approximately 11,700.

Appendix IV: Newspaper Reports, 1943

By January 1943, Germany was having serious doubts about how safe her soldiers were throughout Norway, to such an extent that the thought of an invasion by Allied forces was a strongly held belief.

The *Daily Record* dated Tuesday, 19 January 1943, included the following article:

Falkenhorst Orders 'Fight to the Last' If Norway Invaded

German soldiers in Norway have been ordered that in the event of an Allied invasion they must fight to the last man and contest every yard of ground.

The order comes from General von Falkenhorst, the German Military Commander in Norway, who told his men: 'We all have one duty, to fight to the last bullet and the last drop of blood in the strongest and most fanatical resistance.'

Feverish preparations are being made to counter invasion. Falkenhorst recently ordered the erection not only of more coastal fortresses but of strong points inland.

In Oslo and Bergen, preparations have been made for street fighting.

The greatest fear for the Germans in Norway is that their sea line may be cut, thus leaving them alone to their fate.

Special measures have been taken by the German authorities to conceal the extent of the RAF raids on Berlin from the Reich army of occupation in Norway.

Browned off soldiers were told in a broadcast yesterday that the attempt to break the morale of the nation by raids, especially that on Berlin, had failed.

Details of the striking three point protest against Quisling persecution read in most of the 1000 churches in Norway on Sunday, have become known in messages from Norway to Stockholm.

In January 1943 there was genuine belief of a forthcoming Allied invasion of Norway by the German High Command, fuelled in part by mention of such a possibility in the Turkish Press.

In the *Nottingham Journal* dated Saturday, 30 January 1943, was a small article on this very matter:

General Erkilet, in Cuin Huriyet, considers it probable that this will be opened to pave the way for other fronts in France and Greece.

Moscow radio stated yesterday that fresh German troops 'have recently arrived in Norway' and that many houses in a number of coastal towns have been turned into strongly fortified points.

The theme of an Allied invasion of Norway showed no abating and by February 1943, the press had almost gone into overdrive on the matter, as more articles on the topic continued to fuel the theory. Fact or fiction, it was certainly something high on the agenda of the German High Command and their troops in Norway.

Tuesday, 9 February 1943 saw an article on the subject appear in the *Daily Record*:

Two-sided invasion of Norway feared

The possibility of a two-sided invasion of Norway by the Allies was hinted at in Quisling newspapers yesterday.

The danger can arise either from an extension of the Russian offensive or of British and US action against Northern Norway and Petsamo, says one statement.

Other reports discuss the possibility of a Russian attack against Kirkenes and the Varanger Fjord near the Russian Artic border.

One newspaper claimed that RAF attacks against the Northern Norwegian province of Finmark have lately been greatly intensified and that a number of communities there have been destroyed by bombs.

The *Daily Record* kept up its coverage of news on the situation in Norway, with an article which appeared on Monday, 29 March 1943. Whether the newspaper actually knew it or not, the contents of the article it printed were extremely accurate, as by that time large numbers of men from the SOE had already arrived in Norway via the Shetland Bus:

> Norwegians in Stockholm said today that an entirely false picture of the situation in Norway was given by the report in a Stockholm newspaper that 500 British secret service agents and about 500 Norwegians had been dropped in Norway this winter and were now awaiting the signal for action. The numbers were unknown to all but a very few.

Unconfirmed German claims of a victory over a large force of British and Norwegian parachutists at Hardangervidda appeared in British newspapers on Tuesday, 6 April 1943. One such report was included in the *Evening Despatch*:

It is claimed in today's German communique that in Northern Norway a sabotage force was engaged while approaching the coast and wiped out.

The German controlled news agency in Stockholm recently reported that British and Norwegian parachutists had established a headquarters at Hardangervidda in Western Norway.

According to the Swedish Press, a hundred Norwegians from the Flverum district near the Swedish frontier, had been arrested by the Germans.

Thursday, 6 May 1943 saw the *Belfast Newsletter* include an article about Norway's resistance during Germany's initial invasion of her country. This had come about as a result of a talk given on the topic by a member of the Norwegian government:

The courage and devotion of the people of Norway in their resistance to the German oppressor were topics dealt with by a prominent official of the Norwegian government in London when he addressed a public meeting in the Great Hall of Queen's University, Belfast, last night.

Mr Stanley Wright, who presided, recalled that he was in Oslo when the Germans invaded Norway. He made his escape into Sweden, eventually reaching Britain. Norway's resistance to the oppressor, he said, had never wavered.

The lecturer, after dealing with the German invasion, emphasised that the Allied forces had inflicted on the Germans casualties much heavier than had generally been supposed. Some 60,000 Germans had been killed on land, while many more had been drowned.

> While the struggle on the part of the Norwegian people
> was waged unflinchingly, no sections of the community
> had worked with greater zeal and devotion than the
> Church and the teachers.
>
> The present situation, the lecturer said, was extremely
> tense, the people longing for an Allied invasion, at the
> same time appreciating that events must take their course.

To some degree the article shows just how effective the Norwegian
resistance, ably assisted by elements of the SOE, who had been
ferried into the country via the Shetland Bus, had been. To have
killed some 60,000 German soldiers was no mean feat.

An article appeared in the *Sunderland Daily Echo and Shipping
Gazette*, dated Wednesday, 23 June 1943, which told of a 'catastrophic'
rise in disease in Norway:

> A catastrophic onset of epidemics in Norway is one of a
> series of reports received in London today, says Reuter,
> pointing to the spread of disease through occupied
> Europe.
>
> The Nazi Health Directorate in Oslo, it is reported
> from Stockholm, has had to admit the prevalence of the
> disease due partly to malnutrition and reduced powers of
> resistance, and partly to hygiene difficulties. The number
> of medical cases in Norway in a single month rose to
> 55,000, an increase of 70 per cent over the previous year.
>
> Cases of diphtheria increased from 516 to 1,062, and of
> tuberculosis from 256 to 314. Venereal disease, which had
> practically disappeared in Norway before the war, has
> made serious strides.

Such issues were a major problem for the Norwegians and greatly
affected their lives in numerous ways. There was concern for the

individuals actively taking part in the resistance movement. If too many of them were affected by any one of these diseases, the effectiveness of Norway's acts of resistance against the occupying German forces could have become a major issue.

It was also around this time that Generaloberst Falkenhorst, the German commander-in-chief of German forces in Norway, had cause to leave his headquarters in Oslo and make his way to the country's northern districts, due to a number of incidents of unrest among his men who were stationed in garrisons in the area.

The following article appeared in the *Birmingham Daily Post*, dated Tuesday, 6 July 1943. It was a brief resumé of two books written by Norwegian authors. The first was entitled *They Came as Friends*, by Tor Myklebost, and the other was *Nazis in Norway*, by Ake Fen.

Both of these books on Nazi-occupied Norway insist on the long period when the Germans genuinely expected and attempted to win sympathy for their New Order, and Norwegians at home tried hard to accommodate themselves to the German regime. Not till halfway through either book does one come to the period of open resistance and open terror.

Mr Tor Myklebost, now Press Attaché to the Norwegian Embassy in Washington, is clear and impressive in his account of the earlier methods of the Germans and the way in which all sorts of Norwegian institutions, Labour, the judiciary, the Church tried to make the best of a bad job, even with king and government in exile. He does not defend this policy, but merely shows how it was made almost inevitable by Norwegian faith in democracy and in the general reasonableness of man. He does emphasise, however, its result. When the 'home front' was formed, it was a united and very effective front. Germany's plan was bound to fail, because the very most she could offer a proud, prosperous nation was a humble and unremunerated place in the world of the Herrenvolk. Failure was made surer and swifter by the use of Quisling and his followers. Quisling and his followers, too, were responsible for the worst of the 'terror'. The closing pages tell of brutal violence, Norway's sufferings resembling those of other defeated nations. But it is the early pages that are best worth reading.

Mr Ake Fen's 'Penguin Special' tells the same story in rather livelier style though not more impressively. It makes, perhaps, a little clearer the effectiveness of Norway's 'home front', and throws rather more light on military operations.

It was interesting that these two books, both of which had been written on the same topic whilst the war was still ongoing, provided detailed and accurate information about the events taking place in German-occupied Norway.

Despite the fact that Myklebost worked for the Norwegian Embassy in Washington, neither of these books were an attempt at propaganda by the Norwegian government.

The *Lincolnshire Echo* dated Tuesday, 14 December 1943, reported on a joint British and American 'feint attack' on Norway, clearly showing that the Allies had not forgotten the beleaguered nation. Britain, in particular via elements of its SOE, was actively engaged with the country's resistance network, already displaying their commitment:

The 'feint attack' on Norway with a dummy convoy, part of the Anglo-US Navy's 'coat-tailing' operation reported yesterday, was made at the time of the United Nations landings in Sicily.

Arthur Oakeshott, Reuter's correspondent with the Home Fleet makes this clear in a second dispatch which reached Reuter today.

After describing how everything was done to make the enemy show himself without tangible result, Oakeshott concludes, 'But our time, presumably was not wasted. Maybe it caused the Germans to move large forces of bombers from an area nearer Sicily. Maybe it increased the "anxiety complex."

'And it is more than likely that after we left the area, sea and air forces came out looking for a non-existent Norway bound landing force.'

Some five months earlier, on the night of 19/20 July 1943, fifty Russian naval vessels were reported to have been stationed off Vardo in northern Norway, with the Germans believing that they were there to cut off Petsamo and attack the Finnish front from the rear. Germany claimed that the Russians had made three attempts at landing their troops, all of which they had thwarted.

About the Author

Stephen is a happily retired police officer having served with Essex Police as a constable for thirty years between 1983 and 2013. He is married to Tanya who is also his best friend.

Both his sons, Luke and Ross, were members of the armed forces, collectively serving five tours of Afghanistan between 2008 and 2013. Both were injured on their first tour. This led to his first book; *Two Sons in a Warzone – Afghanistan: The True Story of a Fathers Conflict*, which was published in October 2010.

He also has a teenage daughter, Aimee. Both his grandfathers served in and survived the First World War, one with the Royal Irish Rifles, the other in the Mercantile Navy, whilst his father was a member of the Royal Army Ordnance Corps during and after the Second World War.

Stephen collaborated with one of his writing partners, Ken Porter on a previous book published in August 2012, *German POW Camp 266 – Langdon Hills*. It spent six weeks as the number one best-selling book in Waterstones, Basildon between March and April 2013. They have also collaborated on four books in the Towns & Cities in the Great War series by Pen and Sword. Stephen has also written other titles for the same series of books, and in February 2017 his book, *The Surrender of Singapore – Three Years of Hell 1942-45*, was published. This was followed in March 2018 by *Against All Odds: Walter Tull the Black Lieutenant*. October 2018 saw the publication of *Animals in the Great War*, in January 2019, *A History of the Royal Hospital Chelsea – 1682-2017 – The Warriors' Repose*. These last two books were written with his wife, Tanya.

Stephen has co-written three crime thrillers, which were published between 2010 and 2012, and centre round a fictional Detective named Terry Danvers.

When he is not writing, Stephen and Tanya enjoy the simplicity of going out for a morning coffee, or walking their German Shepherd dogs early each morning, whilst most sensible people are still fast asleep in their beds.

Index